IT'S ME, BASYA

TNS

Copyright © T N S
All Rights Reserved.

ISBN 979-888591436-9

This book has been published with all efforts taken to make the material error-free after the consent of the author. However, the author and the publisher do not assume and hereby disclaim any liability to any party for any loss, damage, or disruption caused by errors or omissions, whether such errors or omissions result from negligence, accident, or any other cause.

While every effort has been made to avoid any mistake or omission, this publication is being sold on the condition and understanding that neither the author nor the publishers or printers would be liable in any manner to any person by reason of any mistake or omission in this publication or for any action taken or omitted to be taken or advice rendered or accepted on the basis of this work. For any defect in printing or binding the publishers will be liable only to replace the defective copy by another copy of this work then available.

<u>Dedicated to:</u>

Sringeri Shararadamba

Udupi Sri Krishna

Hanuman ji

Last but not least,

My lovely Mom and Dad

Contents

Foreword

"Nanu Nanena" novel is marvellous. It is suitable story to select for an award or to make a cinema. I had only one answer for the readers of Nanu Nenena who were asking why you can't give rights for cinema? Or why you can't send this for selection of award?" That is: Currently I am living in Malaysia. It's been more than two years I came to Bangalore due to Corona. Though few of my cinema director friends had asked to send this for award or to give cinema rights, I need to definitely come to finish the required procedures. Due to the current corona condition and flight travel restrictions, this required procedure is bit delayed. Definitely this might come as a cinema in future. Let's wait and see."

But, from the advice given to me from one of my friend, it really made me to think a while. "What if I don't do this as a cinema? It can be translated to other languages, right? The novel combines Village life, city live, military, love-lust-romance, pain-happiness, human relationships and all of these with equal amounts of philosophical finesse and definitely has the plot and quality to translate into any Indian language, including English. So he gave advice to get converted. So I was like, Yes right? This did not click to my mind all these days and I started working on this aspect.

Indeep Sri Chayapathi Ramaswamy and Navyashree helped in translating to English, where Sunanda Gautham helped translating to Hindi. With their help my first novel "Nanu Nanena" has been translated to Hindi and English. All the gratitude of my efforts should go to them. Thanks a lot to them for translating so beautifully than I expected.

I am keeping this novel which is converted to English in your hands. Bless me. All the characters and situations in this novel are just fiction. Please give your feedback for its characters and scenarios.

- Yours

TNS

03/Feb/2022

mailme@suresharao.com

www.suresharao.com

Preface

Myself Navyashree from Bangalore. Basically I am Kannada and English translator and I am a voice over artist too. By chance I met Suresh Anna (TNS) on facebook and our introduction started with exchanging of our professions. The interaction started in a very interesting way where he proposed me to translate his book to English. I was bit hesitant in the beginning as a translator, giving life to the translation as the author, is not an easy task. But he was like; you can do it, and why cant you try doing it. Then I was motivated so much by his encouragement and with the help of my uncle Chayapathi Ramaswamy, we completed this translation. I will be really glad if you like our work and atleast we are near the essence of the author's writing. I humbly say that I am very grateful to TNS for giving me this opportunity and I pray god to bless him, his family and all his writings, with name and fame as an author.

-Navyashree S G

"Hey Basya! Get up I say! Lazy fellow! Sun has risen to the mid-sky and your still sleeping! Get up! Collect the cow dung, clean the cow shed and draw the milk. Get up I say!"

No; My ears which were more attentive towards the mother nature, did not listen to the utterance of aunt. My eyes which were amid sleep could not properly look at her. My mind which was lost in beautiful dreams did not pay heed to aunt's talks. But she would not stop talking. In my sleepy state, I was feeling as if she was talking from a far away distance and as such they were not properly reaching.

This Spring season is like that! It can mesmerize anyone. It can attract the iron from any distance. Then what about me who has spent some twenty years in a place surrounded by nature. The trees, creepers, animals, and birds have had a great emotional impact on persons like me. Every time spring brings with it a new experience. The budding green leaves, cool breeze passing through the leaves, the nightingale cooing to the beauty of nature, king of fruits Mango kindling desire in people and birds with tempting aroma. No poet would find suitable words to describe the Spring mornings, he cannot express his feelings. It is just a unique experience to be felt by an emotional human being from his inner self. The Sun, as if he is eager to listen to the lilting singing of the nightingale, is somehow pushing the Moon away with his bright rays. His rays touching the spring fallen nature, is converting the entire sky with redness, and rising in the sky. Don't know what kind of bondage the Sun rays have with the chicken, the moment the Sun rays fall on it, it gets up from sleep and wakes up people with its Ko – Ko. The cow seems to ask the human beings to get up by saying 'Amba'.

Every Spring season provides me a new experience, new youthfulness, new energy. Though I sleep on the stone which becomes hot with the bright Sunshine, I don't feel the tiredness. The rock near the house serves as my bedroom. The cowshed is my palace: The Bhairava Hill where I lead the cows for feeding is my workplace. My friends Thimma and Sanya also come here to feed their cattle. We leave the cattle by themselves and spend our time in swimming and playing. Within seconds of sleeping on that rock, I slip into deep sleep and by experiencing the thrill of touching the mother nature, I feel a great amount of warmth and comfort. But for the alarm of the chicken, my sleep is not disturbed by anybody else. With the cool breeze hitting my body and the aroma of mangos from Shanbhog's farm touching my nostrils and cows, nightingales' sounds serving as lullabies, I was forced to sleep for some more time. How could a poor guy like me belie the wishes of mother nature? I slipped into my sleep once again.

"Get up I say! I am howling for a long time now. You are sleeping like a bull. Lazy fellow! At what auspicious moment your mother gave birth to you, I don't know! She died by handing you over to me. Eats bellyful three times a day and sleeps like Kumbakarna, get up - lazy fellow!"

I am not sure whether I was asleep – or whether I was awake. Without my knowledge, I started shedding tears. Yes. It was true that I was asleep; it was also true that I was awake. It was my mistake. But why should she scold my mother for that? Reluctantly I got up and prayed "Karagre Vasathe Lakshmi...." My mother had taught me this shloka and had inculcated the practice of chanting it every morning after waking up. It is said that Goddess Lakshmi, Saraswati and Gowri reside in our palms! If it were true, why Lakshmi hates me so much? With this thought I cleaned my tears and got up. Yes, as Aunt was screaming, Sun had already risen above the head. But not here, may be some country like France, America or somewhere else. I have heard that when we have burning Sunshine here, it will be the evening in some other country: thinking so, I got up. But at least half an hour is due before the Sun could properly rise. To put it in simple terms – it was just quarter to five in the morning. This was like Sun reaching the mid-sky in my aunt's style of speaking! Got up from the rock, walked towards the cowshed through the inside of our house. Having gone through the ritual of waking me up so early in the morning, as if it was her prime duty, aunt had already started snoring! From the water tank, I took the cold water and washed my face with which my sleep totally disappeared. I cleaned my teeth with a charcoal. I saw what is called as Colgate Toothpaste, by using which I was told the teeth will become sparkling white! I decided to use it once, next moment decided against it thinking that aunt may scold me if she sees using her paste. Dried my face with a dhoti and entered the cowshed.

*****

Our place is called Chandapur. As the name suggests, it is truly beautiful. On the other side of our plain land is Madhugiri hill and this side, it is Pavagada hill. The entire region is surrounded by several hills. There were hardly about twenty houses in our place. I would not be wrong if I say that there are more hills than the houses. On the one side nestles Bheema Hill – They say that Pandavas during their Vanavasa visited this place once and rested on this hill. Since then, it is popularly known as Bheema Hill. On the other side is Rama Lakshmana Hill. If we go a few yards beyond that, Hanuman Hills is situated. The rock located next to Rama Lakshmana Hill is known as Sita hill. Besides, there are Kyathe God's Hill, Gowda's Hill, Karta -Veeryarjuna Hill, Navagraha Rock, Silver Pallakki Patil's Hill – so on and so forth. From the top of the hills, we could see our houses which were appearing like red covers. Though ours was not a malenadu, we were blessed with opulent rains. The red tiles on our houses did have the strength to withstand the rains which were lashing continuously for one or two months in a year. Though there were stray incidents of few tiles giving in to the forceful rains, the coconut feathers, gunny bags and plastic sheets were used to protect from the rainwater. With the presence of so many hills, will there not be rivers? Some spring which was originating from the Bheema hill was taking the shape of a river and was passing through the right of the hill, merging with Vasanthi river and was passing towards God's Hill. During the heavy rains, sometimes, Vasanthi river was roaring threatening to submerge our houses. All said and done, wasn't Kala Bhairava sitting atop our Bhairava Hill our village God? Can Vasanthi play mischief in front of him, to whom Deva Ganga herself has surrendered? Bhairava was protecting our place by ensuring that Vasanthi does not enter our area. My age was not ripe enough to analyze the stories narrated by my grandmother. Our place, it appears, was a forest earlier. A great saint called Chandrananda Swamy was living in that forest. The saint, dedicated in the service of Bhairava, was climbing the hill at the sunrise, offering pooja to Bhairava and meditating there. I am told that he was meditating by standing on one leg. Something called plague mother attacked the Bhattara village situated at a far away place and took the lives of everybody. Those who could escape from there, started living here. When the saint was offering pooja to Bhairava, these people were also joining him. During a monsoon, Vasanthi was flowing dangerous and started taking all the routes. The saint was washed away in the flood which angered Bhairava – who in turn cursed Vasanthi. Vasanthi, realizing her mistake, prayer before Bhairava to show mercy on her. Bhairava, it appears, was satisfied with her prayers and ordered her not to flow in this place any time in the future. Since then, Vasanthi does not flow in our place. How many stories like this my grandmother would narrate? Once she would narrate historical, next time philosophical; after that Ramayana – Mahabharata, If she tells me Thenali Ramakrishna's story one day, next day I will have the pleasure of listening to Panchatantra stories. Grandmother was an encyclopedia of such stories! Listening to her stories, I would sleep on her lap and soon slip into a deep sleep.

*****

After washing my face, I got into my daily routine. I collected the cow dung put it into the bin, cleaned the shed and looked at Kamadhenu. A sense of satisfaction. Kamadhenu is the most wonderful creature on this earth. The only self-less animal on the earth from head to toe. It tolerates the violent behavior of the human being and considers serving him is her only motto. Whereas the human being! Besides the flesh and bones, the body is full of selfishness, pride, arrogance. What kind of service we render to mother cow? One bunch of dried grass and little water. And, what do we expect from her – milk, curd, ghee. When she licks my leg out of affection only one question comes up in mind – how do I payback for her great service to us? Hey man, I hate you for your selfish attitude.

I swept and cleaned the shed, kept water for her, drew milk and came inside the house. I get thrilled to look at the cream floating on the fresh milk. Returned to the shed, untied the calf and allowed her to go to her mother. The scene of the calf drinking milk and the mother cow licking her child really excited me. Besides the mother Kamadhenu, wasn't it my mother who took care of me without any selfish motive? How much she struggled for my sake? When I was suffering from some strange disease, she carried me on her shoulders and walked such a long distance for my treatment. Would I be in this pitiable condition if my mother was alive? Without my knowledge, few drops of tears ran down my face. I washed the shed once again. Approximately one and a half pots of milk. I poured it into the new can and started towards the diary.

"You idiot, add one more quantity of water I say! Don't carry the thick milk" – Not sure whether aunt spoke in her sleep itself or I myself recalled her everyday dialogue. What would I lose, I added three more mugs of water, tied the can to the cycle and started towards the diary.

While coming out of the diary Hussain Sab told me "Hey Basya, disbursement money towards milk supply has come, ask your mother to come and collect". Thinking that she was not my mother, she was my aunt I rode my cycle towards the house. Hussain Sab is a rich person in our place. He runs many businesses like Milk Diary, Kerosene Shop, Ration Shop, Big Market in the adjacent village, Millet Mill, Poultry Shop and so on. I have heard that MLAs who visit our village during election time, meet Hussain Sab in his hour. Don't know the connection between MLA and Hussain Sab. But he has given the contract to construct a bridge across the Vasanthi river which connects our place. All that is fine. But why did he call aunt as my mother. Is it not ten years already since my mother passed away? At that time, my father married this lady thinking that someone was needed to take care of me. Is not she my aunt, doesn't Hussain Sab know this? Why can not he give the disbursement amount to me? No faith in me? Yes they don't believe me – Not Hussain Sab, but aunt. She may fear that I would take all the money and run away to some city. Who will take care of the cattle? That's why she has ensured that I don't get access to any money. But, I will not give up. One day or the other, I will run away from here and settle in the city. Shetty, Patil from our place keep frequenting the city. Its much bigger than our place. People who go there will get the job. Five-six storey buildings, car and tv for every house. Yes! I will also go. Today or tomorrow, I will go to the city! Anyway I want to become a police or join military. I can fulfill my dream if I go to the city. In this thought, I rode the bicycle, reached home, parked the cycle against a pole. Not sure whether it was prepared last morning or night, a ragi ball was awaiting me. After consuming it, I left for cattle feeding.

*****

I will be completing twenty years on the coming Sri Ramanavami. I was born in this Chandapura house itself. My father Bangaraiah was a music exponent in our place at that time. For all the stage plays in thirty four villages surrounding our place, my father was invited to be the teacher. This doesn't mean that my father was highly educated. He completed his education in the Primary School in our village. He possessed enormous talent though he had passed only fourth standard – this was the gift of my grandfather Bhujangaiah. His accomplishment in the field of music was far greater than Gowrishankar mountain. Perhaps my father inherited these skills from his father. Starting with small concerts, he rose to the level of rendering his voice in big events. My father was presenting musical concert during Bhairava Fair at the time of Shivaratri. There used to be a fairy tale that Bhairava used to adorn the chariot only on listening to the music of my father.

Like my father, my mother was also a great devotee. Saraswathi – a name synonymous with the Goddess of Vidya. When it came to the matter of patience, my mother was far superior to Saraswathi. She was managing all the household works of the family starting from sweeping, swapping, cooking, serving the food, cleaning the vessels, washing the clothes and many more. We never notice the signs of tiredness or disappointment on her face. I am told that I was born six years after their marriage. At a time when they had given up all the hopes of getting an offspring, I had come in their life to continue their family tree. The entire village was fed with special food. Though my parents were not very rich, they were not poor either. With a land of four acres, they were growing enough rice for the family and guests. As the cow was giving enough milk, there was no dearth of milk, curd, ghee in the house. We were not selling any one those things as my father was dead against selling the things blessed by Kamadhenu. My education was completed in the house itself. When mother Saraswathi is residing in the house, where was the need to go to school? When the head of the family was a treasure of music-literature, which greater teacher than him was needed? Right from childhood, my mother taught me the significance of education. Day, Star, Panchatantra, Ramayana stories, devotional songs on Chamundeshwari, Parvathi and other Gods and Goddesses were taught to me. Though I was a boy, I was trained on the skills of preparing the flower garland, cooking, putting rangoli etc. I was also trained in music by the teacher of thirty four villages. Though I could not master the art of music, I learnt to enjoy the feelings of it. When I joined the first standard in our Primary School, I was five and a half years old.

One and a half years from there, the death of my mother who was my guru, inspiration, my life everything. The news had come as a thunder to me when I was studying in the second standard.

*****

After eating the ragi ball, completing the cattle feeding, I went towards the Bharava hill. After entering our School compound and reaching the other side, Bheema hill was situated. The black rock seen in the opposite direction was Hanuma Rock. If we cross Rama-Lakshmana Rock, Seetha hill, and proceeded further we reach Bhairava Hill. I remember mother telling me that Rama-Lakshmana-Seetha were sitting on the hill to relax, this place was called Rama-Lakshmana-Seetha hill. When there was a fierce battle between Bheema and Hanuma, the rocks thrown by Bheema became popular as Bheema hill and rocks thrown by Hanuma was called as Hanuma rock. Bhairava hill is seen at a distance after crossing the Lakshmana rock and passing through the forest area. I left the cattle after reaching the Bhairava hill and looked around. My close friends Thimma and Sanya had not come. I washed my hands and feet at the pond, took some flower and offered it Bhairava inside the temple. I prayed to God and sat singing the songs taught by mother.

Shiva Shiva Sambasadashiva
Oh Bhairava the protector of our place
With a request to forgive our sins
Standing before you with folded hands...

By this time, Sanya reached the place with his cattle.

"Hey Basya, what are you doing?"

"Nothing I say, here I come", I came out.

"Hasn't Thimma come?" I asked him. It seems Thimma's child is not feeling well. He brought the child to our house. My father gave medicine for three days. So, he is at home taking care of his child. "Ok, leave it", saying so we went towards the pond to swim.

Me, Thimma, Sanya – all three of us are good friends. Our friendship is more than ten years old. We will be together from morning to evening every day when we come for cattle feeding. After we leaving the cattle for grazing, we would roam all around the place and there is no place which is not touched by us. We would go around hills and rocks, mango farm yard, swim in the big pond, take a nap at Bhairava's temple and would return only in the evening. We would also play all traditional games including Kabaddi. Don't mingle with Sanya, he belongs to lower caste, aunt was shouting at me often. I was pondering what has the caste to do with friendship? No. My upbringing did not permit me to distance myself from Sanya on the pretext of caste. Sanya was younger to be by four or five years and his moustache was just budding. Though he was younger, he was built well. No one would imagine that he would climb the tree with such a hefty body, but he was quite fast in the same. Besides, he is quite familiar with different types of trees in the forest. People in and around our village knew that Sanya's father was giving treatment for snake bite. Wherever the snake bite would happen, whatever time it may be, he used to rush with service mindedness. Sometimes Sanya also was accompanying his father. During that time, Sanya's father used to brief him about the different qualities of various trees. There were times when Sanya himself would go, collect the plants and other ingredients from the tree and prepare the medicine. Though he has not mastered the standard of his father, he was preparing the medicines to the acceptable levels. But Sanya would never show such medicinal plants and trees to us. He would make us stand at a faraway distance and he was fetching the leaves. As we had heard that the medicine would not work if we saw its preparation by hide and seek.

Thimma may be elder to me by about one or two years. Though he was not fair looking, he was not at all having the black complexion. Attractive physique. It may be already five or six years since Thimma was married. His is a beautiful family – a cute child. I used to visit his house every now and then. I was spending some time in playing with the child. But since they were not allowing Sanya because of his caste, I was also not feeling like going alone. If Sanya was good in tree and monkey game, Thimma was good at swimming. So to say, it was Thimma who taught me and Sanya the skills of swimming. As we had not learnt in the initial stages, Thimma used to push us in to the water forcefully, with the sole intention of making us learn the skill of using our hands and legs to swim naturally. Gradually, we started to swim by ourselves. Of late, I had become a master in swimming and was even able to defeat Thimma too. Thimma was not just elder to us by age, but also, he was ten times more practical and experienced, perhaps due to working in his father's stores. But I know Thimma from his childhood. Highly intelligent; accurate accounting; precision in his measurement of items, speaks only when it was required; ability to defend his decisions. Wasn't he even rescuing us within no time whenever we were on the verge of being caught while stealing mangos or tender-coconut? Today, me and Sanya decided to swim ourselves as Thimma had not joined us.

That time, I was just about seven years. Though I was studying in the second standard, I was able to teach the entire school. Academic curriculum those days was not like today's bookish texts. They were systematically teaching us the alphabets, grammar, sentence formation etc. Details like Star, Day etc., were also taught to us every day. Introduction of the historical cities of India, states of India, capital cities, culture, and tradition in different parts of the country were explained to us. As I had learnt the skill of mathematics at home itself, I was made the monitor of the class. If anybody made any mistake in star, day etc., I used to correct them. Besides all classes from first standard to the fourth were conducted in a single hall and Muthanna was the sole teacher for all the classes. Even the syllabus was the same for everybody. I used to guard the classes and students in the absence of Muthanna teacher and was scolding them whenever they created any nuisance in the class. I was writing such names on the black board and the teacher was punishing them with his stick. Many students used to bribe be with ginger peppermint, guava fruit etc., expecting the favor of not writing their name on the board. Many of them were complaining to my mother saying that they were beaten by the teacher as I had wrongly written their names. Embodiment of patience, mother used to listen to them patiently, advise them and made them to play with me. Sometimes, she was even offering food and consoling them.

Father had gone to Hyderabad with some drama company about four days ago. Mother and I were at home. Mother seemed to be very tired. "Son, I have fever and I will not eat today. Come I will give you food", saying so mother gave me food in my palms, cleaned the vessels and made me sleep. She got up in the morning, after sweeping and swapping she woke me up. By the time I got up, put rangoli in front of the house, gave grass to the cow, cleaned the cow dung and drew the cow milk, she had prepared hot rotis for me. After completing the breakfast and picking up the slate, I looked towards mother for the chalk pencil. Mother looked at me as if to ask, "Did you use the chalk pencil given yesterday or ate it yourself?" I was standing still. Looking at me, mother could not control her laughter. She gave another piece of chalk pencil and kept the remaining part for tomorrow. I ran towards the school in one breath.

That day, Muthanna teacher was explaining about the planetary system. The enormous power of the Sun, planets moving around him, the process of day and night etc. Muthanna teacher's teaching was not just like a lesson, it was like a story telling. He was making effort to recreate the scene in the minds of his students. He was saying that the distance between each planet would be crores of miles! The distance between our village and Narasapura is one and a half miles. How much a crore would be like? Oh... So far? What would be the distance between the Sun and the last planet? He was asking these questions by himself and providing the answers also.

Just then, Sannegowda came and whispered something in his ears and returned at the same pace. The teacher removed his specs and asked me to go to him. I thought that Sannegowda had complained to teacher against me because myself and Thimma had pelted stone to his dog yesterday. Cursing Sannegowda, I continued to sit in my seat. The teacher came near me, hugged me tightly and started crying. Nobody understood what happened. After a few minutes, the teacher asked everybody to go home and declared a holiday to the school. He held my hand and walked towards my house. By the time we reached home, Gowda, Patel, besides few ladies had gathered there. When I was thinking why all of them have come there, the teacher told me "Not from the backdoor, let us go from the front door". As we entered the house, Thimma's mother came rushing towards me and started crying holding me tightly. She told me reluctantly "your mother passed away I say". What do the mean by 'pass away?'. All that I understood was 'my mother has gone away somewhere and will never return'. Thinking of this, I started crying loudly. Patel was instructing people to this and that, call for the priest etc.

*****

"Hey Basya! Look, Thimma is coming", Sanya who was sitting atop the tree shouted loudly. I felt as if I gained some new energy. When everybody in our village goes for cattle grazing to nearby places, why should I go only to Bhairava hill? This question had haunted me hundred times. We were going there because we could speak openly only in that place. We would forget the whole world and spend our day freely talking, singing, swimming, sleeping.

"Hey Basya! Who don't you go to city! You have very good voice! You can earn good name in music just like your father did. Thimma had told me this several times. Yes! I also feel the same way, particularly whenever aunt was torturing me. But the moment I think of going away from a friend like Thimma, I forget that idea. Thimma had become an inseparable part of my life. The moment Sanya announced the arrival of Thimma, an enthusiasm suddenly arose in my mind. "Child was not well, now he is better. That's why I came; come let us swim" he called us. Nodding our head in agreement, myself and Sanya followed Thimma. On the way, Sanya was advising Thimma about the ailment, medicine to be administered, what is the magnitude of the ailment etc. Besides, he climbed some tree and brought some leaves. This was the first time Sanya prepared the medicine in front of us. I asked him "hey Sanya, the medicine doesn't work if you prepare it in front of others, isn't it?" "Hey, nothing like that I say, these are all trade secrets which you will not understand", saying this he looked at Thimma and Thimma too started laughing looking at me. "Nothing I say, the child is too small you know, so it works. It does not work for elders if we prepare the medicine in front of others", saying this Sanya laughed once more.

I don't understand anything. I did not have the practical knowledge like Thimma. Not that I did not have, I did not need it also. I worry about myself, my work, taking the cattle for grazing, eating whatever aunt gives me, sleeping and getting up. This was my limited world. Music was another asset of mine which was keeping me lively. Though I had not mastered the art of singing, I had the melodious voice which would suppress the mistakes that I would commit in my singing.

Thimma was advising me frequently to go away to some other place to escape from aunt's oppression. He thought I could build my life using the skill of music. Where will I go, who is there for me? Aunt may scold me, beat me; but she gives me food regularly. During the night, I get a peaceful sleep looking at the sky. How will I get food in a strange place? Where will I sleep? So, what if I don't get food, God who has sent me to this world will ensure my food also. What kind of life I am leading here? By my age, Thimma had already married, and he had two children. Here, I don't have the freedom even to dream! Sangeetha Saraswathi has graced me, and I can surely make good use of it. If mother was alive today, I would have surely performed one or two concerts by now. Yes! I should go away to the city one day or the other. I should become a great musician. No, no, no... I don't have to become a musician. Don't I know how much suffering my father experienced because of the music. He is wandering from place to place. Not sure whether he is dead or alive. I should join the police force or the Military and then return to my village. I am told Police can beat anybody. I felt like becoming a policeman or a Military person, return to our village and take revenue on my aunt.

*****

Today, somehow, I feel very much tired. So, decided to return home early. Don't feel like swimming also. No enthusiasm at all. I told Thimma that we will return early. He also agreed. We changed into our normal dress and came in front of Bhairava temple. For some reason, my wavering mind was fully of anxiety. I sat crying and just looking at Thimma and Sanya seeming to ask them 'what next'? Not able to open my eyes, I just rested against the tree. Thimma and Sanya were both trying to console me.

I am not able to digest the fact that my mother, who gave birth to me and who went on to become my teacher, friend, and philosopher, who was everything to me in this world, was not there with me anymore! Though I was too young to understand the meaning of death, I went on crying. What is the difference between my mother's death and people of the village assembling in our house? Mother had told me once that those who die will go near the God. Does it mean that mother has gone near the God? Why would not she return? Would Bhairava send my mother back if I pray to him? Like this, hundreds of thoughts were passing in my mind. Not able to understand anything, I was just leaning against a pole, quietly watching the developments there. Tears were flowing endlessly from my eyes.

"Not known where Bangaraiah is now, it appears that he has gone to some far away place with the drama company. Not sure where he has gone and when he would return. I have given the information to Drama Artist Jakkappa, if he comes to know about Bangaraiah he will tell him" Thimma's father told Patel. Then what to do next was the question on their face. Thimma came straight to me and sat down. "Nothing will happen I say, take courage, all of us are there with you", he consoled Basya. The moment I saw Thimma, I felt a sense of satisfaction and my crying and tears took a short break.

Patel told someone to shift mother's body onto a mat. Two persons lifted her body, turned it and placed it on the mat. The priest who had just then come from a bullock cart was getting the rituals done by chanting some mantras. Since I could not understand anything, my hands were mechanically performing as per his instructions. Without being aware, I lit the pyre on which my mother's body was lying. I experienced convulsion either due to the heat of the burning fire or due to empty stomach. I don't know when I regained my consciousness. Thimma was sitting next to me. His mother was using a handmade fan to help me get some breeze. It was a truth that without my knowledge, my future life shifted to Thimma's house.

*****

What I say? Being a grown-up man, you are afraid of that lady. Let us go home and see what does she do? What does she think of you? You are not a bonded laborer in that house. Let us go, I will also come. I will take her to task. Sanya was murmuring whatever he pleased like. Yes! What Sanya is saying is right. Why should I be afraid of aunt? This is the house where I was born and the only son of the house is like the owner of the house. What right has she got to dictate terms for me? When this house, money, property, land everything belong to my father and grandfather, why am I fearing like a bonded laborer? I looked at Thimma acknowledging that Sanya's words were correct.

"Hey Sanya, keep quiet I say. Don't talk like an immature person. Just think over. He is not a bonded laborer. But that lady is his father's wife, isn't it? Which means, he is her son. Can the son quarrel with his mother? Even his father is roaming around the places with the drama company, because of his fear about her. When that is the case, what can Basya do? What will you do if she says that this is the personal matter of her family and asks you 'who are you to interfere in this?' Being a quarrelsome lady, she will summon the Gowda, complain against you, and see that you are thrown out of the village. Control yourself. I am thinking what to do next. Somehow, I also felt that Thimma was right. "As it is she behaves like a Shoorpanakhi. If I tell her that Gowri is lost, will she keep quiet? She is fond of Gowri of all the cows. No cow in their shed gives as much milk as Gowri. She will not spare him if he tells her that such a cow is lost. Basya, listen to me. I have been telling you from the beginning to go to the city and take up a job. Please listen to me now at least. Please tell him Sanya", Thimma repeatedly advised me. Sanya also nodded his head in affirmation of what Thimma had told. At that moment, I saw Thimma in the form of Lord Krishna who preached Bhagavad-Gita. He gave me some money for my expenditure. I thought that my bondage with this village is over. I prayed to Bhairava from wherever I was and left.

*****

Somehow, consoling words of all those who were present there appeared to be sympathy towards me. It was enough for them to say a few words and leave the place. I was feeling disgusted towards the relatives who are feeling as if their duties and responsibilities were over. Though young, I could make out the difference between the true love and sympathy. I feel nauseating to hear the words 'orphan, poor guy, small boy etc.' That's when I saw Thimma as a brother and a friend. He does not have an iota of selfishness. Indeed, he was an inspiration to me which enabled me to come out of those sympathizing people and give shape to my own personality. If I had not earned his true love, I would have perhaps become mad in mother's memory. God decides the relatives and leave the choice of friends to us. Otherwise, I would not have met Thimma!

Thimma's mother was preparing tasty food and serving me. She was not discriminating between Thimma and me. She was consoling me, tell the stories and making me sleep. Next day morning, it is the same amount of love. She was telling that mother had gone to the God, she was pleased by my works. She was making Thimma and me sleep on her laps by narrating stories about heaven and hell. Though I was little embarrassed during the first few days of my stay in Thimma's house, gradually I had adjusted myself to that environment. I had all the freedom in his house.

Father returned probably after ten fifteen days after mother's death. He came to know about the news through Gowda and cried by hugging me. I had never seen father getting so emotional. A man stronger than the steel had suddenly become softer than cotton. Gowda, Patel consoled my father 'Teacher, you have to advise us, instead of that you are crying like this. You perform dramas in places, preach Bhagavad-Gita to people and now you are not able to control yourselves. Whatever was to happen has happened. God likes the good people; he does not recall the sinners. Look at the condition of your son, fill some courage in him." Father wiped his tears, held me like a child and brought me home.

It appears father did not sleep the entire night. He had enquired everything about her death, me performing the last rites, rituals etc. He also came to know that I was having my food in Thimma's house. Amid all this, something struck his mind which did not occur to me at all. I had not gone to the school since about one month. He had made arrangement to send me to school from the next day. This helped me to return to normalcy with studies, school, friends, teacher etc. My father was taking care of cooking, washing the clothes and vessels and all those works which were handled by my mother. Even amid his busy work, he was not missing music and drama practice.

That day, I saw my mother in father. There was no closeness between me and him who was roaming around the places with the drama company. He used to come home once every twenty or thirty days. Only myself and my mother were in the house. But ever since mother passed away, I did not see father going out of the house at all. He was taking care of all the works that was done by mother till now. As I had grown up eating the food prepared by mother, I did not know the cooking skill of my father. To tell the truth, father's cooking was in a way tastier than mother's preparation. While he was cooking, I was sitting outside and practicing music or taking care of my studies. But mother was not like this. She was giving me few works like cutting the vegetables, cleaning the vessels etc., so that I learn to manage the house and share the workload. Though I had learnt to giving finishing touches after observing her cooking, I had not developed the confidence of cooking by myself. As I was not liking the idea of sitting outside when father was cooking, I was entering the kitchen and helping him. In the beginning, father was telling me not enter the kitchen as I was still young. Gradually he stopped his objection and allowed me to help him. At a very young age, I had learnt cooking, doing household works, cleaning the vessels besides cattle grazing, managing the cow shed etc.

*****

Holding Thimma and Sanya, I was walking towards the other side of Bheema hill. Synonym with the name, Bheema hill was quite steep. Few days ago, three of us took the challenge of climbing the Bheema hill and alighting but lost the challenge and returned half-way. But where did we get the courage of climbing it with ease today? We haven't eaten, feeling tired. But we are determined to climb the hill. I am not afraid of snakes, scorpions, and thieves. My sole aim was to reach the railway station situated on the other side of Bheema hill. I had the ambition of seeing the train by a close distance at least once in my lifetime. But I did not imagine that I would get an opportunity to travel by the train so soon. All that was before me at this moment was to board a train, reach the city, take up a job, earn money and return to my place. With that ambition only, I demonstrated the courage to climb the Bheema hill and reach Byadarapalya. Climbing the hill looked too small in front of my dream of going to the city. Man can achieve any thing however big it is, if he has the zeal and enthusiasm to achieve something in life. Had not mother once narrated the story of Dhruva? Wasn't it the inspiration for my mission today? I gained the confidence that if I could climb Bheema hill, I could conquer any force in the world. I was elated at seeing the Byadarapalya Railway Station. I feel like laughing loudly and dancing. Having climbed the hill successful on empty stomach, now I am sensing that I was very hungry and thirsty too. Hence, I slept on a nearby rock.

"Hey boy who are you I say Why are you sleeping here?", I heard someone shouting at me. Though my eyelids tried to open forcefully, I could not do so as I was very tired of climbing the hill. "Hey boy, I am talking to you only", hearing the voice again, I opened my eyes and looked around. Pitch dark all around, stars sparkling in the sky. I had never come out of my house in the darkness. I was frightened at the darkness, but gaining courage sat up. The person standing in front of me was staring at me only. Hey boy, I am asking you only, where do you want to go? Why are you sleeping here? He repeated his questions.

"When will the train to city come?" I asked him.

"What?" he asked again as if he did not understand what I asked him. Fearlessly I told him "I want to go to the city. I want to become a policeman; I want to join the military". Don't know what happened, he laughed loudly and kept on laughing for some time. I was just looking at his face. Why is he laughing like this when I told him that I want to go city? Doesn't the train to the city come here? Have I come to a wrong place? I developed doubts in my mind. He stopped laughing and said "Oh, this is such a case. I have seen many people like you who have gone to the city in search of jobs but have returned disappointed within three days. Go home, eat food and sleep". "No, I will go to the city, and surely earn money" I told him boldly. Looking at my boldness, his laughter stopped. "The train comes at night three o'clock and goes to Bombay. It takes four days to reach Bombay. What will you do for food?" he looked my face. I did not think of all this in my urgency to catch the train. I looked at the little change I had in my hand. "Hey boy, why do you look like that? You will get food in the train. When the train stops, you will get peanut, cucumber at stations. Don't worry about anything but be careful. There will be thieves who will deceive you. Don't eat anything offered by the strangers. Doesn't matter if you spend money, buy, and eat. Do you understand? You appear to have suffered too much in life. Take this... for your food. I also don't have anybody. No wife, children. Take my son, keep it with you", saying this he forcefully kept some money in my pocket. I had left the house fearing aunt. A person whom I had not met in my lifetime earlier is helping me like this. Oh God, what is your miracle? Waiting for the bench I sat on a bench.

I was feeling sleepy because of the tiredness of climbing and alighting the hill. But I forced myself to be alert and awake so that I don't miss the train while in sleep. God only knows if I miss a train, when will I get the next one? He said that the train comes at 3 o'clock in the night, what is the time now? How long should I wait? Will the train come from that direction or this? A boy who was dreaming of seeing the train, is travelling by train, that too for four days! How luck I am. My good days have started – like this I was lost in many thoughts. At last, I could hear the siren of the train from a distance, and it was coming towards me. Wow! How long it was! What speed! What majesty! It bears the capacity to transport thousands of passengers from one place to another every day! Speed of a lion! Within few minutes slow speed like a tortoise! How far the train would have travelled on the rails so far? From where the train gained so much energy to carry thousands of passengers?

Kooo...train's siren itself was quite reverberating in my ears. At what speed it could be running now? Why are the trees, hills, rocks, and buildings moving backwards as the train moves ahead? Where are these many people going? Why? Are they going to the city or somewhere else? Is the train full of people today or is it like this every day? What is the time now? At what time will I reach the city? My mind was wandering back and forth like a pendulum. Though I was feeling sleepy, I decided to enjoy the train journey. I came to the door and sat on the footsteps. The train was travelling the whole night. My mind was full of enthusiasm for the first time in my life. Enthusiasm had overtaken the tiredness. Breathtaking scenes of nature on either side, roads seen at a distance appeared like rangoli, agricultural fields with paddy and sugarcane, beauty of the scene when the train was passing through hills and bridges! Wow! It is simply inexplicable. After a long time, I am experiencing such happiness. I laughed last when my mother was alive. Afterwards, laughter did not come anywhere near me. The moment I remembered mother; tears started rolling down my eyes. I wiped my tears, washed my face, and returned to my seat.

Dirty sleep! When required it does not come near me. When I don't want to sleep, it keeps troubling me. Despite my best efforts, I could not sleep. Did I not feel like sleeping in the railway station a short while ago? Now the train has come, I have sat in the train, but why am I not getting the sleep? Is this not the first train journey in my life, I am heading towards an unknown place, in such a situation how would I get the sleep? So, I sat near the window looking at the outside world. What could be distance between my village and the city? How many rivers, lakes can be crossed without swimming? The river which I saw few minutes ago was so long! What could be seen at an infinite distance. How many villages and cities the train was passing through and how many people were there in those places? All relatives – mother, father, aunt, uncle, grandfather, grandmother all of them were finding a contented life there. Why was I denied of all these? Thinking like this, I leaned against the window. Even the God would be disturbed at my condition. But are we not his puppets? How do I know that there would be a bright life ahead of me? My eyes closed to the cool breeze, and I slipped into sleep. Train continued its journey.

In the morning, I looked around once from my seat itself. The hills-rocks, trees and plants are moving backwards, no... the train is moving forward. I don't remember an occasion where I would have woken up without the aunt's morning prayers "Hey Basya, get up I say". Now there is nobody to scold me. There was a tap next to my seat. I was wondering over its presence inside the train. Hesitatingly I went there and washed my face. All the people were in deep sleep. The moment cold water hit my face; my tiredness disappeared completely. After washing my face, I returned to my seat. Slowly, one by one woke up and washed their faces. Looking at the movement of people, I understood that there was a toilet inside the train. I also completed my morning rituals.

"How far is the city from here"? I asked the person sitting next to me. Perhaps he did not understand what I spoke, so he asked me "What?" in Hindi. Not being able to understand his language I turned towards the window and sat quietly. The train slowed down and stopped at some station. While some passengers started alighting, others on the platform started boarding the train. By that time, one vendor came inside with Idly, Coffee, Tea. Anyway, I had little money with me. I paid some and bought Idly and chutney. While eating the idly, I remembered "Wasn't it the last time when I ate idly when mother was alive?". I bought two more idly and ate them.

Ticket, ticket. Ticket please madam, ticket please sir. Announcing this a person came inside. I thought he had come to catch those who had not purchased the ticket. He shook me by my shoulder and demanded the ticket. I murmured "That, that... no ticket." "What, you don't have a ticket? Come, come you - ticketless traveler. Nowadays, people like you are increasing in number. Do you think train is your father's property? I will hand you over to the police in the next station. You will learn a lesson then" he threatened me in Hindi. I don't know what happened, I fell at his feet and begged "I have made a mistake, kindly excuse me Sir. Please don't hand over me to the police. Please stop somewhere here, I will get down. Not being able to bear the torture of aunt, I am going away to the city. I should go to the city to join the Police Force or the Military." Saying like this I started crying loudly. I don't know what he felt about me, he softened his stand and told me "Ok, its ok, get up; don't cry". He took out a ticket from his bag and gave me "please take this, this train does not go to Patna (as I used the word 'Patna' to mean city in Kannada), it goes to Bombay. Keep this ticket with you, if anybody asks show this to them" saying this he went to the next passenger. Though he did not understand my language, he had sensed my feeling. I kept the ticket in my pocket, wiped my tears and sat in my seat. Those who were watching the development all this while returned to their respective seats. I was left with little money and the ticket. I gained further courage and made a resolution in my mind "nobody can stop me from going to Patna... no Bombay". The train accelerated its speed and moved towards Bombay. Don't know whether it took three days or four days, the train reached Bombay. On my part, I was deeply satisfied with the train journey.

*****

2

Seeing thousands of passengers alighting and boarding the train as soon as the train came to a halt at the Bombay Railway Station, I got down from the train. Stepping on to the platform, I saw the scenario all around me once. How will be my life in this bustling world? How? Moreover, where would I go now? Thinking of these hard realities, I started walking towards the exit gate. People were entering and exiting through the large glass door which I thought was the way to exit and I was right in my understanding as the door led me to the outside world. Immediately, I found the world there to be weird. Thousands of people, followed by taxi, horse cart, rickshaw drivers, infinitely visible skyscrapers, hotels with heaps of a variety of strange eatables. I am an orphan without any purpose and direction in this big city where I did not have anyone who could be called mine. Anyhow, I have reached Bombay. Where will I go now? Will I get a job in this massive city? What about my food if I don't get a job? Though chikkamma was scolding me, I never starved of food. Now, what next? I don't know why, for the first time, a sense of confidence had developed inside of me. "Almighty will ensure my food" was the favorite statement of mother. Let's see what happens, God is there, with this faith I started walking again. The city appeared endless as much as I walked. Not sure whether it was a town or city. Was not aware which direction I was walking towards. Large number of people were seen all around. It was a bustling world. Burning sunshine. When I was going for cattle feeding in remote areas of the village, I used to sleep under the shade of some tree. The sunshine was so much scorching. Oh God! Tried everywhere for water to quench my thirst. Are there lakes, rivers in this Bombay city? Went inside the nearby Tea stall and sat there drinking a glass of water. A boy came near me, appeared to be a steward, stared and asked me "Kya Chahiye?" Though I did not understand his language, I asked him in my language to give me a packet of biscuit and a cup of tea. After eating the biscuits and finishing my tea, I paid him the bill and peeped into my shirt pocket. Few changes were still left with me. Though there was no problem for food for one or two days more, my immediate worry was where would I sleep? Once again, I prayed the God and continued walking. Though I roamed around all the roads, small lanes, there was no sign of getting a job. Or, I was not in a position to explain them in a way they could understand my situation. I did not understand their Marathi and they did not know my Kannada. I decided to wait for some more time as I had little more money with me. As the dusk gave way to darkness, a sense of fear started to haunt me gradually. Whether by paying money or by begging, food was not a major worry for me, but where would I sleep? With this thought only, I was walking. As the night dawned, the Bombay city started to change its appearance. Dazzling lights everywhere. Though it was already dark, the movement of vehicles was still quite rapid, Cars-Scooters. Sirens from the Police Jeeps could be heard every now and then. Among the blanket-clad people sleeping on the roadside were Rickshaw drivers, horse cart riders, hotel stewards. The moment I realized that I was not the only one without parents in this city, I got a sort of consolation. I stretched myself in front of a nearby shop and slept for the night.

*****

Its already three days since I arrived in Bombay. Whatever little money was left with me was completely exhausted for food alone. Now I don't have money for even my food. Was it not last afternoon that I ate two chapathis? What shall I do now for my food? I feel as if I am dying of hunger and thirst. Going out somewhere is not possible as there was burning sunshine outside. Don't even have enough strength to stand up. Shall I beg? Oh no! Isn't the mother observing me from heaven? If she sees me begging, how much pain it may cause her. My hunger is not greater than causing sadness in her. Somehow, I took a lot of courage and using all the strength I was left with started walking. No! Was not possible any more; I could not take even one more step further. All of a sudden, I remembered my mother and cried to my contentment, kept on crying. As my hunger increased, my love for mother, her memory started multiplying. So was my hatred towards chikkamma. I cried and sat down taking the support of a pole. I was feeling like vomiting or giddiness. The burning Sun above was continuously increasing my thirst. The tongue was desperately waiting for a drop of water; even saliva was not producing in the mouth to swallow. Continuously I was experiencing giddiness. The body which was roaming around the streets with courage till yesterday, has accepted the defeat by now. I don't know for how long I was sitting leaning against the pole. Passersby on the road continued to ignore me as if they did not notice me at all. Alas! Don't these people have an iota of kindness left in them? Or, are they fed up of seeing hundreds of persons like me every day? Don't know. I had fallen down unconscious.

After a longtime I gained consciousness. I opened the eyes and looked around. Could not make out where was I. Again, looked around. Felt some nauseating smell. Felt like vomiting. I recovered slightly and looked around once more. Yes, it was like a liquor shop. I recovered myself and sat up looking around me. The moment I sat, a boy of my age came and sat in front of me. He assured me through his look not to be afraid of anything. Brought me a glass of water. Where was I? Why did I come here? Who are all these people? Is it really a liquor shop? Is this water or liquor? Shall I drink or not? These thoughts came to mind one after the other. Without bothering about these things, my hands had already picked up the glass and drank the water. I felt as if I had regained my life. He also brought two chapathis and kept in front of me. Tired of hunger at that moment I felt that those chapathis were like amruth. Immediately after finishing the chapathis, I felt a sort of new energy in me. I got up, looked around and started walking few steps. Soon I realized that it was surely a liquor shop. Just like the Puttakka's liquor shop in our town. But I never imagined that there could be such a big liquor shop and so many people could be there. Staring at me, he told "Arey, kya dekh rahe ho, andar chal". He held my hand and dragged me inside and told "Saab! Saab! Yeh Zinda Hai". A stout person sitting there came near and asked "Kaun Ho Thum". I did not know what to tell him at that moment. He asked again "Kaun Ho Thum! Hindi Nahin Aayega"?. No. No reply from me. I did not know what to tell him. I cried loudly and told him while crying "I don't understand your language Sir. I know only Kannada. Don't know anything else Sir. Saying so, I started crying again. I was not sure whether he understood what I told or not, but he understood the word Kannada. Oh! Kannada speaking person, is it? He went inside and brought one more person. That boy came near me and asked, "Do you know Kannada". Wah! I felt that I gained rebirth hearing his words. "Yes sir, I know. My place is Chandapura. My chikkamma was always scolding me, beating me. So, I left the place and came here Sir" I uttered everything in one breath. He explained whatever I told him to his stout person in Hindi. Both of them were speaking something for some time, afterwards the stout person left the place. He turned towards me and told "He asked me to find out from you whether you will work here". They will give meals, breakfast, place for sleeping everything. Some money will also be given, will you work". For a moment I felt very bad. What will my mother feel if I work in a liquor-shop? But, what will happen if I work in a liquor shop? Anyway, I don't drink the liquor. It is just my work. That day my father had advised me that we should not feel bad to do any work. I was worrying if I don't do this work also, how will I eat? Reluctantly, I nodded my head giving my consent. How would I know that the liquor shop which spoils many families, opens its door of luck for me?

****

My new life started in Bombay. It is not just the life, but the lifestyle also started changing. Seena was not just my co-worker, but also, he was my teacher, relative, friend everything. He had taught me the difference between village life and city life, difference between liquor shop and wine shop, my city and Bombay, language of those people, their behaviour and every other aspect. He was teaching me Hindi every now and then. He spoke to his owner and bought me two sets of Pants and Shirts. I was unbelievably looking handsome in the pant and shirt. He knows all the 33 skills of speaking with the customers, taking the order, supplying, scribbling the bill, cheating etc. He taught all of them to me. Still the owner seems to have instructed him not to allow me to go near the customers till I was properly trained. Thus, my works were limited to cleaning the glasses, preparing fried rice in the kitchen or arranging the bottles. There was no dearth of food. We were waking up till 2 in the night and after finishing the work we were sleeping together. Within the next few days, the owner observed my enthusiasm to work and entrusted me the work of taking orders from the customers.

Seena's real name is Srinivasa. Some village near Mandya. Like me, he had also lost his father and mother in his childhood. His maternal uncle's son had called him to Bombay. He was running a Pan shop in Bombay. So, he got a job for Seena with a known Wine Shop owner. Seena became a supplier because of his active handling of the work. Attractive salary besides sufficient tips. Probably because he was working with a smile always, everybody had developed affection for him. Few regular customers would specifically ask for Seena for their service. Even the owner would affectionately call him 'Beta, Beta' implying son. Though Seena was elder to me by ten or twelve years, he was reminding me of my childhood friend Thimma. In a sense, Seena had filled the void created by the absence of Thimma in my life. Due to my association with Seena, my life was literally undergoing a transformation. I was no more an ordinary village boy, but language – dress style had changed me without my knowledge. English words like please, sorry, thanks were freely coming out of me quite frequently. I had developed friendship with my other co-workers too. They also considered me a noble-minded friend. Whether it was due to their trust or confidence in me, they were sharing all their personal problems with me, and I had never let them down anytime. I was never sharing my problems and difficulties with anyone. My principle was to share other's difficulties, if possible, and not to disturb their mind by burdening them with my problems. I had become close to some of the regular customers. Seth ji, Vikram Bai, Basheer Bai, Kapoor ji and many others were very fond of me. Though they were enjoying my crude Hindi, Basheer Bai was silencing them by mildly reprimanding them. Basheer Bai it seems was from Hyderabad. Its over thirty years since he came to Bombay. He owns a big shop near the Central Market. He was appearing in the Wine Store every night exactly at eight or eight thirty. Sab ji, Vikram Bai, Kapoor ji were coming only after nine. Basheer Bai was whole heartedly chatting with me during that time. Though he knew that I come from a difficult background, he was not asking much about it. I was also not sharing anything. Another reason for showing my love for Basheer Bai was his tips. Yes, the tips given by Basheer Bai in a month was itself amounting to my one week's salary. In short, my problem for food and clothing was solved for the time being. Basya who was busy in Cattle raring in the village had adjusted himself to the city life. On the one hand, chikkamma who was scolding me during every meal. On the other, my wine store owner who was affectionately telling me "Eat well, my son". Stomach-full of food, continuous workload, handsome salary, affectionate friend Seena – all these had kindled a new enthusiasm and energy in me. Despite all these, I was sometimes crying thinking of my village. Seena was consoling me in those moments. I don't know why, the moment he spoke to me, I was regaining a new energy. Bombay had given everything that I wanted, except swimming which I like the most. Though I was feeling disturbed over the smell in the wine store in the beginning, gradually I was comfortable with it. I was feeling like blissfully swimming, forgetting the shop, customer, bill everything. Once during my conversation with Seena, I asked him that I wanted to swim and whether there was any well, lake etc. Laughing loudly, he told Oh fool... where should we get lake and well in this city? But, don't worry, I will take you to the swimming pool the day-after-tomorrow afternoon. Ah! There was no limit to my happiness and felt as if the heaven was so close to me! Was eagerly waiting for the day-after-tomorrow! How could I know that day-after-tomorrow would change the course of my future life?

*****

Got up in the morning, finished all my works, had a piece of bread and biscuits with hot cup of tea. My whole mind was imagining the swimming pool where Seena would take me today. When I saw Seena dressed in a new type of tea shirt and a different type of knickers, I felt so happy. We took a horse cart and marched towards the swimming pool. I paid fifty paise more than what was asked by the cart rider. I felt little disturbed after hearing from Seena that we should pay for entering the swimming pool. There is a reason for that disturbance. Let Seena show me the swimming pool today. I thought of coming for swimming every day, even if I had to walk every day. But, what am I hearing now, we have to pay money even to go inside. I was disturbed thinking how I would manage money to pay every day. I recovered quickly from my thought and decided that I can think about that later and for the moment let me enjoy the day now. I went inside, wore a swimming dress and came. I felt little bit awkward and shame. I felt ashamed of looking at half-clad girls and boys swimming together. Seena could not control his laughter looking at my shyness. He looked at me as if to ask 'what Basya, what happened'? When I told him that I was feeling little bit ashamed, he started laughing loudly. Having come to Bombay, you should forego your shame and all that. Look, the girls themselves are swimming like this, why are you feeling ashamed of? There was truth in whatever he told. Bombay city itself is like that. It keeps on moving, unmindful of others with no one having the time and patience to think about others. When I have plenty of problems, why should I think about others? Whatever others may think, this is my life. When I have not cheated anybody, where is the need for me to feel ashamed of looking at others? Immediately I prayed Jai Bhajrang Bali and dived into the water. At that moment, I remembered my village, Thimma, Sanya, chikkamma and all others. No one noticed the two drops of tears from my eyes which mixed with the swimming pool water.

I did not notice the pair of eyes looking at me from the other end of the swimming pool.

*****

A large gathering of people in front of Gowda's house. All of them had only one question in their mind – What happened to Basya? He had not failed to return home even on a single day. But, it is not one or two days, there is no news of Basya even after three days. What happened to Basya? When Basya did not return on the first day, his chikkamma did not bother much. Except Gowri all the cattle had returned home. Gowri must be missing somewhere and Basya must have gone in search of her. She thought that he may be sleeping somewhere there only and returning the next morning. But, no sign of him on the next day also. Let him go to hell, but what happened to Gowri? Of all the cows in the house, Gowri was giving the maximum quantity of milk. When such is the case, how to lose Gowri? When good rate was offered for Gowri during last year's fair, husband did not listen to me. He preached me that Cow is Gomatha, Kamadhenu and should not be sold for money. He doesn't worry about these things, he colorfully speaks to me like this and will spend his time in his own world by touring with his drama company to different cities. It is my fate to worry about all the household works. He is least bothered. If I ask him anything his standard reply would be 'Basya is taking care of cattles, what else you have to do?' Basya is just like his father in qualities. Father roams around different cities and son roams around the streets in the same city. Does not do even one work properly. Keeps on loitering around with Thimma, Sanya. Wastes his entire day outside and returns in the evening to eat like a hog, sleeps till morning. Any amount of scolding does not have any effect on him. What is the use of telling this boy, isn't his father touring different cities without doing anything? If he was perfect, why I had to break my head like this? Has he enquired about my difficulties, problems even once? If I speak up, he silences me by shouting that I am a loudmouth, and he will not live with me. He complains that I torture him by my talks. Let it be there. Where is the loafer? Aah! Mother..., what kind of a son you have given birth to? You left him to my care and died! Husband, wife, son all are thieves! Gowri is not lost anywhere, Basya himself has stolen her! Having stolen, he has sold her to somebody! If so, to whom he would have sold? For how much? Basya doesn't understand these tricks, Thimma must have advised him in this matter! Thimma is a cheat, if I pay money for one measurement of groundnut, he gives me only the three-fourth. Thimma and his father have cheated so many people. They are running their business by simply cheating the people. Because they cheat the people, his child falls sick every now and then. She decided to get the truth from them and knocked on the door of Gowda. Gowda was worried over the news of disappearance of Basya. He called for the Panchayat the next day. Sanya was frightened to hear this news. This lady being a loudmouth may spice up the issue and create problem for us. Thinking like this Sanya ran towards the house of Thimma. Thimma had thought about these things beforehand. He had done brainstorming on what would happen if Basya leaves the place? What all might be asked in Panchayat? On seeing Sanya running towards him Thimma asked "What happened I say, why are you running like this?" "Chikkamma is complaining that both of us have made Basya steal Gowri and afterwards for gaining money we have killed Basya. Panchayat has been summoned tomorrow and I don't know what might happen there. We simply told Basya to leave the place without thinking about the consequence, what shall we do now?"

Smilingly Thimma said "Hey Sanya, I had already thought about these things. I knew that it will happen like this. You don't worry, just say that you don't know the whereabouts of Basya. I will take care of the rest" and whispered something to Sanya. There was a sudden smile on the face of Sanya. "Ok friend, I will do as you say. By the way, how is the child?" "Now the child is better I say, fever has reduced". "Continue to give the potion by mixing it with cow ghee for one more week, child will be all-right, I will go". Thinking about tomorrow's panchayat, Thimma smilingly went inside the house.

*****

3

Having dived into the water by praying Jai Bhajarangabali, I had forgotten myself. As I was swimming in the big lake in our village, I did not like so much the swimming pool situated within the four walls. But, my condition was like a person with a single eye in the kingdom of blinds. Even this was not there all these days. At least this much is there to swim, that is sufficient. I was happy because the dream which I had seen all these days was realized.

I swam, swam and swam. I feel like swimming as long as I exhaust all my energy and become fully weak. Many people were feeling tired in their first round of swimming from one side of the pool to the other. There were a few of them who could swim two to three rounds also. Some of them had come to participate in what was called as swimming competition. They were swimming four to five rounds. But they were swimming with some purpose. Whereas I was doing it for my contentment. To recall the memory of my olden days which I had lost these days. I am swimming to forget the pain within me. So there is no question of tiring myself. In no time, I finished six rounds and started the seventh round. Those who laughed at me when I dived into the water by chanting Jai Bhajarangabali just like a village boy, are all constantly observing me. No wonder if they are considering me as a demon or a specie from a different planet. By the time I swam the seventh, eighth rounds, I was the lone swimmer in the pool. People who were swimming till now have left the pool and are looking at me only. There was a sense of wonder which they might be seeing for the first time. A person who was a laughingstock a few minutes back had become a hero for them. Who is he? Where did he learn to swim? Who is his coach? For which competition is he preparing himself? Probably for Olympics. These kinds of thoughts were passing in the minds of people there. But I was unmindful of all these. I was completely lost in my own world focusing on my swimming.

I did not notice those two eyes looking at me only.

*****

"Silence! Nobody should talk. Please sit down quietly for a minute" as soon as the villagers heard the loud voice of the Gowda of the village, all of them kept quiet. A sense of pin drop silence was created all around. It was as though the entire village had shifted to the panchayat platform. "They ruined me oh God, let them go to dogs! Let him die! Let him get all the sufferings! They have made my innocent son to steal by brain washing him, oh God" that lady's screaming and shouting was at the top of her voice and even the wind appeared to be incapable of competing with her. It is not just the wind circulation, even the leaves in the trees had accepted defeat not able to match the sound of that lady.

"Avva (Amma), Paravva! Please stop crying and explain what happened" ordered the Gowda. Somehow controlling her sobbing, Paravva told - "What can I say Gowda sir, this destructive person Thimma Sanya together have ruined my family! They have sunk our house with their destructive act! Let them go to dogs! Let them get all the sufferings!"

"Why amma, are you all right? Don't instigate me" Thimma also started shouting at her. "Hey Thimma, wait a minute. If you both keep fighting where is the need for Panchayat and us? Wait a minute" said Gowda. "Look at her Gowda sir, what she is saying. She is talking as if all of us have done something" said Thimma. "Yes I say, you have done everything, you have brain washed him" Paravva kept on accusing Thimma. "Both of you control yourselves. If I get angry, it will not be good. We are here to find out what happened and to find a solution. If both of you are fighting like pig and dog, where was the need to call us here"? warned Gowda. Both of them kept quiet by his raised voice.

"Paravva, you have called the Panchayat assembly, tell us what happened. Explain in detail what happened" said Gowda. Controlling her sobbing, Paravva said "What shall I say Gowda sir? Our Basys is not seen since the last three days. Our Gowri also has not returned to the hut. Both these Thimma and Sanya have brain washed Basya, made him steal our Gowri and made him leave the village. My husband is also not there to enquire about my problems. He is touring from city to city with the drama company like a beggar. What shall I do now? Who is there to take care of me?" and started crying loudly. Turning towards Thimma, Gowda asked "What Thimma, what do you say"? "Ayyo Gowda Sir, We don't know anything. He had told me and Sanya many times that his Chikkamma was troubling him because of which he wants to run away from the village. We scolded him, advised him and sent him home. Now, this lady is saying like this. He would have gone somewhere nearby out of anger. Is he a small boy? He will return after one or two days. But we also don't know where has he gone, we don't have the mentality to ruin others' life. Moreover I myself have plenty of problems to look after. Why should I bother about her matters Sir? Is it not Sanya? Said looking towards Sanya. Sanya had slight fear somewhere in the corner of his mind. Realising this without giving a chance to Sanya, Thimma looked towards Gowda and continued to speak this and that. At that moment, Gowda also thought that Thimma also has not committed any mistake. "Look Paravva! We have seen Thimma Sanya from their childhood. They are very good boys. They were accompanying Basya while he was going for cattle feeding. They were going with boys for swimming. Except this, both of them don't have the mentality to ruin others. He would have gone somewhere. After starving for few days, when his anger comes down, he will come back. You don't worry, I will also try to search him once. Also, I will search for your husband and ask him to come home for few days. Till then, you be little courageous. I will tell Siddha to take care of your cattle. You please give Siddha Ragi or something. He will take care of them. Hey Siddha you take her cattle for feeding I say" ordered Siddha. Thimma looked at Sanya and both of them left the place. Thimma Sanya heaved a sigh of relief thinking that they have escaped. Somehow, Gowda had an element of doubt in his mind about Thimma Sanya.

*****

I was feeling as if it was ages since I swam last. I continued to swim to my heart's contentment. I did not realise how many hours had passed. As I was deriving mental satisfaction, I also started to feel the tiredness in my body. Not once or twice, about nine rounds had swam in the pool. Others were frightened thinking that I was from a demon's family and left the pool for my use. The entire pool had become my empire. Even Seena was also frightened to observe my capacity. At last, when I started to feel the tiredness, I stopped the swimming, came out and sat on the edge. With the mixed feelings of happiness, excitement, joy overpowering me, I was confused what was my exact feeling at that moment. On the one side, I was feeling as if I had lost something, on the other I was thrilled for having gained something. One moment I was experiencing hundred mixed feelings, the very next moment, I was without any feeling. Totally, I was in a state where I could not realise who I was. The moment I came out of the water, others started getting into the water one by one. They were seeing me as a special person of extraordinary power.

"Over Sir? Are you happy now"? asked Seena. He was the reason for my brimming happiness. I hugged him strongly and expressed by gratitude. He was also very happy. Wow, what a stamina? Great Man! A man of around fifty years came near me and shook hands with me. Though I could not understand what he was saying, I could understand his feelings. "Congrats great! You are great! What a wonder"! Saying like this, many people came near me and shook hands. Whereas Chikkamma considered me a person who was a lazy fellow wasting 24 hours on swimming, in the eyes of the people I had become a great person. I have some talent in me. The inner feeling that the world will recognize that talent today or tomorrow itself had filled me a lot of enthusiasm in me. A coach who was there came to me and was asking something in English mixed with Hindi. Seena was answering his questions in Hindi. I did not understand what they were talking about. After some five minutes the coach shook hands with me again, said "OK man, see you later" and disappeared. Seena had become a hero that day because of me. When so many things were happening around me, I was observing those two eyes only. Those eyes were also looking at me. After some time, we came out of the swimming pool, took a horse cart and went towards the bar. How would I know that those two eyes which were observing me will be the eyes that would change the course of my life itself?

*****

Within few days, my Chikkamma had returned to normal condition. Siddha was coming everyday and taking the cattle for feeding and was supporting Chikkamma in her difficulties and happiness. Thimma, Sanya also were coming frequently and enquiring about Chikkamma's well-being. Chikkamma who was earlier was shouting at Thimma was quite comfortable with him now. Thimma, all said and done, was a business-minded person. A miser by nature, he was getting pepper, cumin, groundnut oil etc. from his shop and giving them to Chikkamma. This itself is testimony for Thimma's love for me. Gowda had told few persons to search for my father and had promised Chikkamma that they will bring father one day or the other. As a result of medicines given by Sanya, Thimma's child also was recovering from the ailment. Totally, the normalcy started to return in our family. Thimma, Sanya were frequently offering pooja in the temple praying for my well-being. Nobody knew that an incident which the nation will witness with excitement will happen in a few days' time.

*****

My routine life resumed from the next day. I was fully engrossed in the work inside the bar. Our bar owner also had come to know that I had swam for hours together. Not only that, but our regular customer Kapoor ji also asked me "What my son? How was the swimming"? and smilingly patted me on the back. Seeing all these compliments, I became much more enthusiastic about what I had done. I started working at greater pace that ever before. I got the energy to take care of half of the customers myself single-handedly. Owner also was very happy over my performance. I came to know that few customers had expressed good views about my work with the owner. Our owner immediately from that day raised my salary by two hundred fifty rupees per month. Besides, admiring my passion for swimming, he sanctioned one full holiday in a week. There were no bounds for my happiness. I earned a new meaning to my life which was confined to four walls of the bar. One day in a week will be a full holiday. The excitement of swimming the whole day to my heart's contentment, on the other hand increased salary of two hundred fifty rupees had increased by happiness multi-fold. Now, I had two reasons to visit the swimming pool. One full holiday in a week.

Another reason – Those two eyes which deserved to me seen again and again.

*****

In a faraway place called Betta Halli, someone seem to have seen my father. They went to him and explained whatever happened. My father, who had come to Betta Halli along with a drama company, after hearing the incident took the permission of the Manager of the drama company for going to his village for few days. When father was getting ready to leave that day after the night show, the Manager compassionately spoke to my father 'Ok, please go and come. You are the only one who has not gone home for a long time. Please go and come, your son will surely come back. Everything will be fine. God will take care of everything." While leaving he also calculated the earnings for all these days and gave six hundred rupees to my father. At last father came to my village after many days.

Chikkamma, who used to shout at everybody always, had become little bit cool. My father was happy that she was not irritating him or scolding him so much. Still, she was crying in front of my father accusing of ruining her life. As my father was quite matured to his age, he was not breaking is head so much over Chikkamma's talks.

One day, father visited the residence of Gowda. Gowda ordered his wife "Sir has come, get some butter milk" and started speaking. With initial discussions about the drama company, experiences with the company, familiarity with weird people, humor etc., the talks started focusing on me. "Basya is a very good son sir. Once when I forced Thimma to tell the truth he explained everything. After losing Gowri, he feared facing your wife. Hence, he ran away from the village. You don't worry, your son will surely return. He is a good boy. He does not cause harm to anybody. Young blood, he has gone away from home. He will return one day or the other, don't you worry" consoled Gowda. "By the way sir, what if you go away to your drama company after few days. Do you think your lady will spare Basya if he returns in your absence? Please think over this now itself. Make him the owner of the house and whatever land you have. Afterwards, there will not be any problem. Just think over," said Gowda. "I don't know Gowda sir; I don't understand these things. You are a learned person; whatever you say I will do like that," said my father. Immediately Gowda started to act on the same. It was decided that house, land, cattle would be transferred in the name of Basya and till his return Siddha will take care of all these properties for which he will be given some money and grains. Gowda's precautionary measure and his experience led to Chikkamma's screaming once again. "I have been made a beggar; let them all perish". Chikkamma who was silent for few days again started using foul language freely. Sensing the trouble, father again left home for resuming his service at the drama company. Before leaving, he did not forget to meet Gowda once again and remind him to request his kind attention towards his home and land.

*****

"Hi how are you? I am Shefali" I turned towards the person who uttered these words Yes. They were the same eyes. For many days now, those were the eyes which were hunting me during my every visit to the swimming pool and I am meeting the same pair of eyes today. Who is she? I was becoming restless not being able to understand what she was saying. I don't remember having spoken to any girl in my life other than Uma. What shall I speak to this girl now? I was experiencing a sort of shivering. My entire body was trembling. I changed the direction of my eyes, which were till now continuously looking at her, towards the sky. At that moment, there was complete silence from both of us. Breaking the silence, she continued – "Hello man, I am talking to you only". Just then Seena also came and joined us, and I gathered some courage see him. "Sorry madam, he is a Madrasi. He has come from Bangalore and he doesn't know Hindi" Seena told her. She replied "Is it so? I know Kannada also" and introduced herself once again. Afterwards, Seena and that girl were speaking something for about fifteen minutes. Though the discussions were going on between the two of them, I knew very well that I was the subject of their discussion. "Ok, thank you. See you later. Take care", said the girl and left by her scooter. Seen told me "Ok, let us go". I looked at Seena as if to ask him Who is she? What was she saying? "I will explain everything in detail afterwards, we are getting late for work. So, let us leave" said Seena. We came out of the swimming pool. Usually, I had developed the practice of walking from here to the bar. But for some reason I was tired today. That tiredness was not because of my ten rounds of swimming. On this day every year, I was performing my mother's ceremony and this year I am here like an orphan. With whom shall I enquire? How to perform my mother's ceremony here? Nobody knows my language also – that mental tiredness was because of this thinking. Drowning in this thought, I had swam ten rounds absent mindedly.

*****

Seena also did not talk to me much assuming that my mood was not good. I was all alone for some time. After half an hour, Seena brough some rotis along with dal and rice in a plate. "Please have Basya. You have not eaten anything since this morning. You have swum so much and are tired very much. Please eat". I shook my head to say that I did not want it. He asked "Why? What happed I say, please tell me." Somehow, I could not control my tears, cried loudly. "Hey Basya, please don't cry, please tell what happened".

Today is my mother's ceremony. I was performing it every year in my village. I am not able to do it today. The moment he heard this Basya said "Oho, that's all? Why did you not tell me before? If we give money in Bombay, they will perform ceremony not only for your mother, even to you and me while we are alive. Now, you want to perform your mother's ceremony, isn't it? You eat this and come with me". I thought "what is this person saying? Is performing ceremony a child's play?" But I had a sort of confidence in Seena, he was like Thimma in our village. Besides being experienced, he knows very well about Bombay. He will make some arrangement; I should have told him much earlier. But how will he arrange? Like this many thoughts were passing in my mind. "Hello please eat, let us go quickly". I told him "We should not eat anything before performing the ceremony, we should fast". "If I listen to what you say, that's all. Having swum so much if you starve, we will have to perform your ceremony that's all. All right, come have tender coconut at least," said Seena. "Yes, there is no problem if we have tender coconut", I agreed. Seena kept the plate back in the kitchen by saying "I don't understand all these things, come let us go". "Wait, I will inform the owner and come", he went to the owner and told "I am going out today and will return in the evening. I will supply two extra tables till ten o'clock in the night." There was no problem for me since it was my weekly holiday.

Since I was also tired, we caught a horse cart, travelled for about four kilometers, and stopped in front of a big shop. A small lane by the side of the shop. Adjacent to that was a drainage. We crossed that drainage and a few steps ahead there was a half-collapsed compound, we came inside. We drank tender coconut somewhere nearby and walked for about two furlongs. I was not aware where were we going. Seena and I did not utter a word during our movement. Finally, we arrived in front of a small temple. He called me inside. There was a small house adjacent to the temple – the house belonged to the priest of the temple. He spoke to the priest for which they told something. What I could understand from their talks was ceremony has now become an old fashion. People who are addicted to Bombay life will not have time to think about the ceremony also, leave alone performing it. So, it would be good enough to honour a brahmin with dakshine (offering), lunch, dhoti and shalya and performing Pinda Daana in the adjacent vacant space in the name of the deceased. Though I did not like the idea, I consoled myself by thinking why to ignore even this opportunity. As advised by the priest, we bought white dhoti, shalya, saree, beetle leaves and beetles and other items. After taking bath under the tap, we completed the ceremony within half an hour. The priest, it appears, was from Chittoor in Andhra Pradesh. He came to Bombay ten years ago in search of a job. He had learnt Veda reasonably well and thus by luck secured the job of the priest. He was performing the pooja in all earnestness by chanting mantras in Telugu style. Telugu, Kannada, Tamil people in that area like the way he performed the pooja. As the number of devotees to the temple increased, so did his income. Temple Committee people had got him a small house adjacent to the temple on rent. While returning, Seena explained these things to me. Even he did not know whether the priest was married or not, was he a bachelor? Anyway, I had completed mother's ceremony with the support of Seena. It was already three or three thirty in the afternoon. We returned by walk, had one more round of tender coconut, took a horse-cart and went to the bar. All my body pain had disappeared, and a new kind of energy had developed in me. On the one side, I was contented for having completed mother's ceremony, on the other memories of mother, Thimma, Sanya, father appeared in my mind. About one hundred and ninety rupees were spent totally towards horse-cart, dhoti, shalya, offering to the priest etc. Seena had spent everything. Once inside, Seena left for work. I sat somewhere in corner of the room, mother's memory started haunting me again and again.

*****

"Maava how are you? How come you are here? How is aunti? Is Basya doing fine? Please come let us go home. In our place, sunshine is too burning because of which you have tired. Please come home and have a glass of cold juice" saying this she started walking without waiting for my father's reply. After moving a few steps, when she looked back, my father was standing still in the same place. "Oho, don't you worry at all. Mother will not say anything" saying so she called for a rickshaw. "Rickshaw, come maava sit inside" she made him sit comfortably inside the auto. Autorickshaw started moving towards Kodiyala Bailu. If Meenakshi was to sit quietly without speaking for a minute, her food would not digest. Whenever she was at home, it would like a sparrows' nest with the continuous chirping sound. Though she is younger to me by two and a half years, she more intelligent than me. More courageous too. She is a straightforward girl and would never speak behind somebody. She was telling me every day that I don't talk anything and remain silent like girls. By nature, I was not speaking much with anybody barring my mother and my friends. Even when I was silent like a dumb person, she was not disturbed over it anytime. On the contrary, she was talking like a chatter box. "Maava, this is the house, please come inside" saying so she opened the lock and switched on the fan. My father who was roasted under the scorching sun, found the fan breeze quite soothing. He removed the shirt, washed his legs and face and sat on the floor. "Oho maava! Please come here and sit on the sofa". "Not required my girl, having come from outside, sitting on the floor gives much more cooling effect" saying this father leaned against the wall and sat on the floor. "Please take this maava. This is called Rasna, it will be cold. Please have it and take some rest. Mother will come soon. If you need, drink few more glasses of Rasna. Humidity is high in our place. If you don't drink more water, you will suffer dehydration. Take rest under the fan for some half an hour. By that time, I will cook rice. Cabbage rasam prepared by mother in the morning is there. I will serve you lunch." I don't want lunch Uma. I will relax for some time and leave. Poor girl, why do you take the trouble of cooking now?"

"Maava don't you know my nature? There is no chance of you coming to our house and leaving without having the food. Take rest, if you want, I will switch on the TV, keep watching it" she went inside the kitchen. "Ok, you prepare the food, I will return in five minutes" father started to leave. "Maava, hope you are not leaving without having lunch. If you do like that, I will stop talking to you." "Hey no Uma. While coming we came directly here by auto, I could not buy any flower or fruit. I will just go out and buy the flower and fruit. I will return in a while" father started to leave "Oho, that's all? No flower or fruit is required. Look, there are fridge-full of fruits", she opened the fridge door and showed him. Father smiled at her innocence and said "Oho Uma, you are still young. You don't understand all this. One should not go empty handed to sister's house especially where a child is there. It is not auspicious. If we go empty handed, that house will attract Saturn's trouble. I will just go and come. I will not return without having food prepared by you", saying like this he wore the shirt and his footwear and went out.

Father, who went out, returned within half an hour with a bag full of apple, orange, yelakki banana which his sister was very fond of, one saree, blouse, dhoti shalya besides cream bun, biscuits and bakery snacks for Uma. The moment Uma saw the cream bun she was quite jubilant. Probably she shed a tear or two out of her happiness. Yes. When Uma had come to our house during the summer vacation, father would hardly return home after shopping without bringing cream bun. It was available in only one bakery in the city. She would be happy to have cream bun for breakfast, lunch and even dinner. She had a special liking for cream bun brought by my father. She is like this since the age of five years. Now probably she is fifteen or eighteen years' old. Even now she is the same girl and started crying loudly by seeing the cream bun brought by father. Father consoled her and asked her to eat it. Father removed his shirt, hung it to a hook, washed his hands and legs. "My Sose is not bad at all. She is grown enough to cook food". "Oho Maava, I know cooking rice only, it is not a great thing, it is very easy – One glass of rice and two glasses of water, switch on the gas, two whistles are enough, that's all," said she. She is the same as she was in her childhood. Very active. Thinking like this, he himself served the rice. She brought rasam from the fridge, which was cold, but was all right with the hot rice. Having finished his lunch, father asked Uma "why did you not have lunch Uma"? "No maava, I am not hungry, besides I am full after eating the cream bun". After lunch, father slept on the floor under the ceiling fan. Probably because he was tired or had gone out in the Mangalore sunshine, he slept for some half an hour.

"Maava! Enough of sleep, please get up". Father woke up hearing Uma's voice. Father was very happy after seeing his younger sister after a long gap. Whereas his sister spoke few customary words "how are you, Anna? How come you are in Mangalore? When did you come? Had your lunch?" "Hmm, Saroja, I am fine. I am with some drama company people. The owner of our drama company belongs to some place near Mangalore. He has a coconut farm of thirteen acres. He was coming to Mangalore and told me that thieves have become a menace in his coconut farm. He requested me to get 'yantra' so that he overcomes the problem. As you know, I know a little bit of all these yantra, mantra etc., so I did it for me. As he was coming this side, he called me also to accompany him 'Will you come with me Sir? You had told me once that you wanted to have darshan of Lord Manjunatha at Dharmasthala. Please come with me and stay in my house only. From there frequent buses are there to Dharmasthala, go and have darshan. You have strived and have been striving for our Company and you have not even asked for money anytime. Whatever money we have given you for your service, it is too less. But what can I do? You know about the profit and loss of the company. Let me serve you food for two days in my house, arrange for the darshan of Manjunatha so that a bit of your debt on us is reduced. So, I prayed at the feet of Manjunatha the day before yesterday. I stayed there for two days. Both during the morning as well as in the evening, I had a blissful darshan of the Lord. I returned to Mangalore in the afternoon. In the bus stand, I found this naughty girl. She did not spare me till I came here. By the way, prasada of Dharmasthala Manjunatha is there in the bag, I will give you at the time of Sandhyavandane in the evening," father said.

In the meantime, few girls came looking for Uma. Aunti, isn't Meena at home? Please wait, she will come, she is getting ready. Uma came out of the room and told them "No, today my maava has come from his place. So, I will not come for tuition today, I will not come for even Bharatanatya class. Please inform Sir." Her friends told her Ok and left by their cycles. I will just come, saying so Athae went inside. "Saroja, there are flower and fruits in the bag besides bangles. I have brought clothes according to my capacity. Please don't say no to them, please accept. You should not say no to flower, fruits and bangles, they have come from your parent's house," said father. She agreed and went inside the kitchen. After athae went inside, Uma came and sat beside father. "What else is the news maava? I wanted to ask you – how is Basya"? The question from Uma shook the ground for father. My father's nature was staying firm in any situation. My father who was not shaken even when his mother died, was completely taken aback by the question of Uma who had a lot of love for his son. He experienced some sort of anxiety. My father considered Uma has his daughter-in-law. Somehow, he made up his mind to control himself and not to shed even a drop of tear. "Maava what happened? I asked you only, how is Basya"? Father was finding it too difficult to stay there any longer. Right, I will take leave of you. Our drama company owner is leaving tonight only. Saying so, he wore the shirt, chappal and left. All this had happened by the time athae went inside the kitchen and came out. Both Uma and athae looked at each other unable to understand anything.

*****

Somehow, I am more enthusiastic today than ever before. I don't know the reason. But a sort of enthusiasm is evident on my face. Seena also said the same thing. Don't know, May be. After coming here after leaving my house, perhaps begging was the only path for me. Where was the place for even to sleep? But God's grace – I reached a city like Bombay. Handful of salary in the bar. Good and soft-natured owner. A friend like Seena to take care of my problems and happiness. Heartful of swimming once a week. Moreover, the satisfaction of performing mother's ceremony even while I am away from my village. Without Seena would I have done this? Would I have met Seena but for the poojas performed by my mother? Mother was the backbone of our house which was like nandanavana. Though father was the earning member of the family, it was like - mother means home and home means mother. Her death had struck like a lightning in my childhood. After Chikkamma came, our house seemed to have turned into a hell. There was not a single day when she would sleep without scolding or beating me. She had burnt my hand using the hot thava. She should be taught a lesson. Did I not take the train and reached here with that intention? Mother's words that we should not harm others even in our dreams are reverberating in my ears. But is what chikkamma did right? Yes. I feel like joining the police department and beating chikkamma with a stick. I should become a police force, should join the military – however difficult it may be.

*****

"Hey Basya! The load has come" – Seena's calling reached my ears. I went towards him from where I was sitting. Just then the truck had come and stopped in front of the bar. It was my duty always to collect the crates unloaded from the truck and arrange them neatly in the storeroom. Different types of crates separately. Soda crates in one place, Cool Drinks in separate place in the storeroom, Water Bottles separately – it was my every Wednesday duty to arrange these crates neatly. Before me, one Punjabi boy was managing this work. As he was on leave once, that work was entrusted to me. I had the idea of it would be convenient to arrange different things in their proper places, isn't it? So, unlike the Punjabi boy who was scattering the crates wherever he liked, I was arranging them neatly. Anyhow, there will not be much workload on Wednesdays. So, by spending some two hours extra on this work, I arranged Cool Drinks, Hot Drinks, Water, Soda etc., separately, and neatly. I pasted stickers to identify the items. I gave a new look to the storeroom by cleaning and throwing the wastes of broken bottles, broken plastic items etc. Earlier, the storeroom was appearing full because the boy was throwing around the items everywhere. After I cleaned it, the storeroom appeared quite spacious with some more space left for storing additional items. Besides, as I was documenting the incoming and outgoing stocks properly, nothing could come inside or go out without my knowledge. As a result of this new system, even that Punjabi who was earning a bit extra by keeping duplicate records like the say 'Rama's account and Krishna's account', was forced to stop all his tricks. Ever since the owner asked me to take care of the storeroom and the stocks, the Punjabi was angry on me. He left the job saying that he has secured a new job in a hotel. After arranging all the stocks neatly in the storeroom, sweeping, applying anti-cockroach spray in all the four corners, counted the stock once again, locked the storeroom, handed over the keys to the owner and heaved a sigh of relief.

As the evening started, customers started trickling in one by one. Bengali boy was not well and hence, he did not come for duty that day. As a result, the workload was a bit more. It was around midnight when the work was completed. After eating one or two rotis – dal and little curd rice, I felt a bit relieved. A sort of thought had conquered me all over. Hence, I could not sleep properly. My thoughts were hovering over illusion like I had become a policeman and my chikkamma was standing before with folded hands. "What happened I say? Are not you getting sleep? Stupid fellow" heard Seena's words. Without replying I was looking towards the sky. Yes, whenever I was remembering mother, Sanya or Thimma, I was going to the roof of the bar, spreading the mat and sleeping looking towards the sky. If it rained, I would have taken shelter under the water tank, but I would not return to my room. I would get a thrill looking at the sky. In the dark sky, the moon shining somewhere, all around him hundreds and thousands of stars, if it was true that the dead will become stars, I am sure my mother also would be among one of those stars in the sky. Sometimes, mother had woken me up at four o'clock in the morning and shown me the Dhruva star. How many times I would have listened to the story of Dhruva? I was a small child then. Would not know anything about the sky, moon, or the stars beyond the story. But I am not like that now. I have fairly seen the world. I have mingled with people from different countries, languages, dress styles. My present condition is entirely different. The moon, however bright he is, does not appear to have his own light. He stores the sunlight throughout the day and reflects it in the night. But those stars – Oh! Many times, brighter than the Sun, crores of miles away from the Sun. If they were to come anywhere closer to earth like the Sun, their brightness would be as much as to burn the earth itself! God's creation is great. Plenty of creatures living in the water and plenty of lives crawling on earth. Plenty of birds flying in the sky. It is said that no two creations are similar. Describing the sky and the stars is beyond one's imagination. On several occasions, I have spent time like this counting the stars and slipping to sleep later. Not finding me in the room, Seena came to the room in search of me. He knew very well that I every now and then sleep here looking at the sky. He sat leaning against the tank wall and I asked – "What happened? Not getting sleep?" He shook his head indicating "No" and lit a cigarette. Seena smokes cigarette occasionally. He doesn't have the habit of smoking daily. While smoking he asked me "What is the special today? Looking at the sky Sir?" "Nothing, simply I came up. I remembered my olden days, that's all. Nothing else. I was also not getting the sleep. Its very hot inside. So, I came here" I told him. I asked him "Did you not get sleep?" "No".

Today is my wedding anniversary. Every year, I was going to my place, meeting my wife and coming. In the last three years I have not gone there. That's why I am little bit disturbed", he said. By the way, I did not even know that Seena was married. I had told him everything about me, but I had not asked anything about him. I have not enquired about his problems and difficulties. I did not ask about his native place etc. All I knew was that he hails from a village near Mandya. I felt ashamed of myself – realizing how selfish I am.

Observing my silence, he started speaking. My native place is a village near Mandya. My father is Narayanagowda. Mother Rajeshwari. We had a

Sugarcane field of seven acres. A house built by my great grandfather. I am the youngest in the family. I had an elder brother. A girl near Maddur was seen for him. Soon after the marriage, my sister-in-law started to demonstrate her evil behaviour. It seems she was complaining "I should have married a boy from Bangalore, my father dumped me in this remote place". Within few days, my mother died of some disease. About six seven months afterwards, my father suffered a paralysis. The entire left side is paralyzed, even he stammers while speaking, cannot make out anything. Father was keen to perform my marriage before his death. I was twenty years old at that time. My brother is elder to me by two years. Three years after my birth, a baby girl was born in our family. I was very fond of my younger sister. But she died when she was two years' old following some illness.

As desired by my father, my elder brother finalized a girl from a place near Ramanagar. Then onwards, fight between both daughters-in-law started in our house. I had told my wife to keep quiet no matter ho much sister-in-law scolds her. While going to sleep every day, she used to shed tears complaining that akka said like this and that. After a few days, my wife became pregnant. I had decided to send her to her mother's house. Probably due to the auspicious moment of my wife's arrival in our family, the course case relating to seven-acre agriculture field was also decided in our favor.

It was nearly three years since my elder brother was married. There was no sign of my sister-in-law getting pregnant. Younger daughter-in-law who is recently married has become pregnant, what is the problem for this girl? Ladies in the village started gossiping that the elder daughter-in-law seem to be having some ailment, such a girl has been brought by Narayanagowda. My sister-in-law's anger on my father, on me and my wife doubled. There was no sign of my father's recovery also. One day, my wife slipped and fell into the well in our farm. Nobody knows whether she slipped and fell, or somebody pushed her. When we returned after burying her, the entire house looked empty. To my misfortune, I could not blame anybody. I used to spend time at home only thinking about her. Sister-in-law started scolding me everyday accusing me of ignoring the sugarcane field. Even while knowing everything, father was lying on the bed in a helpless condition. Sometimes I was thinking of running away from the house or committing suicide against a train. But I remained at home just with the sole purpose of taking good care of father till he is alive. I had started to develop a sense of detachment with respect to house, land, family, relatives, and everyone else.

I had to shoulder the complete responsibility of taking care of father. Finally, three days prior to Ugadi festival, father passed away. I became an orphan in my own place and in my own house. I don't know how I lead my life for few days afterwards. I was like a dead body. I was not finding taste in any food. Beautiful wife, baby in her stomach kept appearing in my mind again and again. Once my maternal uncle had come to our place. He also went to Bombay in his young age, opened a Pan shop and had settled there only. I heard that he has married some girl here itself. The moment I saw him, I could not control my tears. I explained whatever had happened. Okay, we will press for division of property and handing over your portion to you, we will call the panchayat tomorrow itself, he said. My problem was not about the property. I did not have the patience to stay in that village, in that house and, I did not have the patience to marry once again. I explained all these things to my maternal uncle. I brought me with him here and got a job in a hotel. About three or four years back, I left that hotel and joined here. Since then, this bar has become my home. If I remember my house or place, I work more and sleep peacefully at night. People of Bombay are not as bad as those in our native place. All of them are busy in their own work. I see a movie occasionally. If I am still disturbed, I will visit the beach. Once in a month or two, I visit the red-light area. Saying this much Seena heaved a sigh of relief.

I never new that there is so much pain inside of Seena who a smiling person is always. I consoled myself that my suffering is nothing in front of many people like him who keep on suffering every day. Hiding all his pain Seena presents himself as the most active person, I thought he is a tremendous character. Even now, while lighting his cigarette I found Seena quite an enthusiastic person. That smile was the secret of his charming face, and his greatest morale was his patience. I was reminded of the words uttered by him. Chikkamma who appears in my story has emerged as a sister-in-law in his story. So to say, Seena has suffered more pain than me. Despite that he does not show any kind of hatred or enmity towards his sister-in-law. He has consoled himself by blaming everything on his fate. On the contrary, I am having vengeance against chikkamma. Even this is also the fruits of good luck or bad luck. In the game played by God, chikkamma has donned a role, that's all. She has acted her part. Now onwards, let me not have any vengeance against her belittle myself. Let me not worry what happens to her. But I will not give up my ambition of joining the military. As if I remembered suddenly, I asked him "that's right, while speaking to me you said something like red-light area, isn't it? What is it? Where is it? What is so special about that place?" Suddenly looking at me he started laughing loudly. "No need to talk. When I go there this time, I will take you also. You yourself see that special" winked at me and went downstairs. I continued to watch the stars and slept on the mat. The characters in Seena's story started to pass through my mind.

*****

No sooner than the elections to Bombay City Municipal Council were announced on that day. Some Code of Conduct came into force. Police had an eye on most of the Wine Stores and Bars. We were not having working till eleven-eleven thirty in the night as it was earlier. Bar was closing as early as ten o'clock in the night. Though we were supplying our regular customers from the back door, that was only a personal matter. Since there was no work in the bar, I was finishing my work by ten thirty and climbing on to the roof and was counting the stars. Though there was no work after ten in the night, from seven to ten in the night we were not get time to breath also. I was tired of listening to the election related dialogues whether this party will win or that party will win. The television set in the Bar hall was continuously playing a Marathi channel. Discussions, arguments, minor fights between the two groups of customers, sometimes going to the extent of physical fights had become daily affairs. First, I don't know Marathi and what can I say about my Hindi! Therefore, my owner had told me not to do supply work and only work in the kitchen till the end of the elections. I was doing small works in the kitchen. A newly recruited Marathi guy was posted to work as a Supplier in my place. Though I had not tasted Chicken, Mutton, Biriyani, Fish etc., I had become accustomed to their spell. We had grown up listening to elder's advice that we should not eat Fish and Meat, is it not a fact that they only have become food for lakhs of people? If non-vegetarians start eating rice and rasam, is the present length of land sufficient to grow enough food for all of them? More land is required, farmers are required, so is it not a balancing act of God? Like this, new thoughts were passing in mind occasionally.

While being a supplier, I was running around a lot. I was talking to hundreds of people. Each one of them were placing different types of orders, bill, change, tips, pepper, salt, cigarette, lighter, tissue paper...Like this there were tens of reasons to keep me busy. Besides, when I had no work, I was watching the TV and sitting on the stairs. But I was feeling bored of this kitchen work. Same vessel, same stove, same orders, same type of work. I was getting headache due to the smoke in the kitchen. The cook was working continuously without a break. Though we were chatting a bit now and then, how could we hear each other amidst the noise of the stove? So, a sort of loneliness started to haunt me. When I look back at my life, I feel that there was no meaning to my life. What did I want to do? What am I doing now? There is no comparison between the two. I just know that I should join the Military force. Where? How? Whom to meet? When will they select for Military? Place? I don't know anything. It appears even Seena doesn't know anything about this. Poor guy: how would he know about Military? Whom to ask? Kapoor ji, Sait ji, Vikram bai, all of them are businessmen. They may say something if I ask them about their business. Of all the things, if I ask them about Military, what would they say? Thinking like this, I was staring at the stars. Without my knowledge, I slipped into a deep sleep.

*****

"Hi! Why are you so dull today? You are not the same as other days today. What happened? Are you still in hangover, are you all-right?" saying so she giggled. "Nothing like that. I am feeling bored somehow" I told her. "Yes, why your friend is not seen nowadays. Breakup? I know about breakup happening with girlfriend, what is this breakup between the boys?" again she giggled. She is correct. Seena is not coming with me for swimming. If I ask, he says, why should I be an intruder. Its nearly two months since Seena came for swimming with me. He is also not interested in swimming. He was coming for my sake. After my introduction to her and after we both started speaking more and more with each other, he had stopped coming. Yes, isn't it two months since Shefali became my friend? How did it turnout to be a friendship? All that she knew about me what that I was a good swimmer. She did not know anything about my village, background, my work etc. It way just hi-bye friendship.

Was it not about two months back? Seena only showed her standing in front of the cash counter in our bar with her friends. Seena had shown her to me and asked "what is this I say? Why has she come here? Has she come in search of you?" "No, no. She doesn't know that I am here. I looked at him to indicate that even if she knew about it, there was no such friendship between us for her to come in search of me. The moment she saw me suddenly, she asked Hi, how come you are here? "I am working here as a supplier. This is my home also" I told her. "Oh, is it so? Nothing, today we have a part in my friend's house. Anyway, there is a cricket match between India and England. So, we thought of seeing the match and having some beer. We have come here to take beer parcel. See you later at the swimming pool" gave a smile and went away. "What is this I say, ladies in our place don't go to shops for buying sugar and coffee powder also, they send the boys. These Bombay girls come to bar to buy the bottles", I said. "Oho fool, where are you, look at the world properly" saying like this Seena went inside.

*****

"Hello! What are you thinking man"? Looked at her and replied "Hmm! I am here only but thinking about something". "OK, come on, lets go and have a Vada Pav" saying so she started the scooter. Within ten minutes, we were standing in front of Mandeep Singh Vada Pav shop near the beach. Yes. After Shefali became friend, we have not missed eating Vada Pav here at least once a week. It has become a daily routine, no weekly routine to have Vada Pav and drink Ginger Tea and chat a lot. Of late, Shefali's Kannada also was becoming more and more clearer. Though she knew Kannada even earlier also, she was finding it difficult because she had no one to speak in Kannada. In the beginning of our friendship, she would not understand my Kannada, I would not understand her Hindi. Now, it is better.

"What are you thinking so deeply? Don't you share it with me even?" she came and sat next to me. Somehow that day I was feeling that she was an intimate friend to me, and I thought of sharing everything with her. I quickly narrated about my place, childhood, chikkamma, cattle, like this I told her my entire life story. Without my knowledge, few drops of tears had fallen from my eyes. She had heard all these as if that of a story from a movie. She would have considered me that day as a strange person. "From outside, you keep smiling so well, do you have so much paid inside you. Oh My God its ok! Come on... stop crying. Take this hand kerchief. It is my responsibility to admit you to Military. I have got a good friend like you; this is the gift to you from my side. Okay? Cheer up" she kept her hand on my hand to reassure me and started looking at me. I also felt a lot more comfortable. I became happy thinking that my dream of joining the military was getting fulfilled. "It is getting dark; come I will drop you" she invited. "No, you please proceed. I feel like sitting here for some more time and watch the raising waves under the moonlight". Okay, bye. Get ready for next week; I have a surprise for you", saying like this she went by her scooter. I sat on the sand, looking at the raising waves from the mid-sea.

*****

"I am really very sorry; it appears you don't have the parameters required to join the military", my eyes were wet at hearing her words. Yes, I had realized my capacity in last week's running and jumping. There was no need for Shefali to express it. The other candidates who had come there were far ahead of me in running, jumping, physical fitness, educational qualification, Hindi – English languages etc. In front of their performance, my running and jumping were like an ant in front of an elephant. What else? All doors to join the military had closed for me. After many days, I cried a lot. With so much crying, my eyes dried, but I could not console myself. God only knows for how long I was sitting there and crying.

"Mr. Basavaraj! Madam is calling you" that person informed me. Shefali and I looked at each other without understanding anything. Madam is calling means... who is calling? She is calling me or you? Or would she have called someone else? He is clearly calling my name Basavaraju, that means it should be me only. It was Shefali who christened me as Basavaraju. We went inside to find out who was calling. There was a small meeting hall inside. Some six to eight chairs around the table. Shefali sent me inside and sat at the reception reading some newspaper. I went inside and wished "Namaste madam". "Oh, namaste Basavaraj, please come and sit" she welcomed me. She was a lady of about fifty years. Her appears itself was indicating that she was in some high position in military. Rough face, height of not less than five and a half feet. She was wearing the military uniform. Not sure whether she was married or not. She seemed to be busy in browsing some files and signing them. "Please give me ten minutes" she seems to have told me. After signing the files, she turned towards me and started to speak.

"So, you are Mr. Basavaraj. I am in a top position to recommend the physical fitness of the candidates desirous of joining the military. While browsing through you file, I got an idea. We are not able to select you to the military as your height and weight are not suiting the military requirements. I am sorry about it. But I have come to know that you are a good swimmer. We have a team called Rescue Task Force Team. This team is dedicated to help the people during earthquake, cyclone, and such emergency situations. We are getting many people who know running, jumping, jeep driving etc. But we are getting a very few profiles of people who know swimming. So, I got an idea whether we can accommodate you in the swimming category. So, I called you. Please go and come back here by three thirty pm. You can have a swimming test. Good luck"! Not sure how much I understood from her Hindi-English talk – but I was feeling as if I was almost touching the sky. A sort of happiness. Though my eyes were dried after crying for such a long time, they could not control the happiness which I was experiencing at that moment. Two drops fell from my eyes automatically. The lady sitting in front of me looked like a Goddess. I was not conscious of the place of my presence. I went straight, touched her feet as a mark of my respect. "Hey, what is this non-sense" she took back her shoe-clad feet. Appearing to me touched by my happiness, tears, humble and innocent behavior, she told me "Go my son! May Jesus bless you", while saying so she touched her cross-clad chain around her neck.

When I came out of the meeting room, somewhere nearby Shefali was sitting and reading the newspaper. She turned towards me and gestured to ask what happened. I ran near her and in a jiffy explained what all had happened. I could see happiness in Shefali's eyes. "Wah great, you have done it' saying these words she gave a tight hug to me. I was so happy that I even forgot to express my gratitude to Shefali who brought me here from nowhere. I was completely speechless at that moment. I folded my hands and told her that everything has happened because of you Shefali." "Oho fool, nothing like that. I am just a friend. My friend asked for help, and I just did it. Nothing special. Come, let us have some tea and come back. The swimming test is at three thirty. You are not just selected. Please remember that they have called you for a swimming test. Come', she said. I told her "Yes, they have asked me to come for a swimming test, I am not yet selected. But one thing is true, they just cannot reject me in the swimming test. Even if the Almighty becomes my opponent, I am sure to win. I have so much faith in my swimming capability". I did not utter these words out of arrogance, but because of the immense faith in my swimming. "I also know that, but be calm now, come let's have tea" she comforted me. We walked towards the nearby canteen.

*****

Wow! Is this a swimming pool or sea? My heart skipped a beat for a moment. Shefali did not allow me to eat anything saying food may make my body heavy. Both of us had a pav-bhaji each with a cup of tea. A sort of new enthusiasm had filled my body and soul. I wore the special dress given by them for swimming purpose. Two gentlemen from the selection committee reached there and each of them stood at both the ends. A coach came and gave me the instructions. This was the swimming pool situated within the premises of military office because of which Shefali was not allowed to come inside for security reasons. As soon as the coach gave me the instructions, I got ready. Besides me, no one else had come for the swimming test. Therefore, I did not take long to realize that it was a test exclusively organized for me.

It was not an easy task to swim four rounds continuously in this pool. Even the coach explained the same thing to me. He gave an appropriate answer to the question why such a stringent test was required. One may have to be in the water for hours together while rescuing people during calamities, earthquake, cyclone, flood, and such other extreme conditions. That too without food and water. If the nature fury was continuing, the challenge would multiply. It is not an easy task to save not just our life and save tens of other lives. During the last year's Tamil Nadu flood, one person called Thomas had saved about ten persons, that too by swimming against the flood from one end to the other. My God! I was thrilled to listen to the coach. I remembered my arrogant words that I would win even if the God became my opponent and felt ashamed of myself. For the first time, I started to doubt my swimming capability. But I considered it as an opportunity provided by the Almighty which I should not waste. I became mentally determined to achieve it and joined the military. It may just be a job opportunity for many persons who come out of overenthusiasm. But it is not like that for me. For a long time now, I had decided that this will be my future life. What value my life will have? Do I have mother, father, brother, sister or relatives or my own house? I am a human being without anything. Thus, my life will be purposeful if I save the lives of some ten persons. Even if I were to die tomorrow, I don't have anyone to shed tears. When such is my life if I could save some lives that would be enough. My mind had become fully determined.

The moment I heard the whistle sound of the coach, I jumped into the water chanting Jai Bajrang Bali. One – two – three rounds, the entire energy in my body had waned. One more round left. Somehow, if I could complete one more round. I decided that there was only one more round to fulfill the dream of my life and with all my energy started for the last round. Oh no, was not possible. Perhaps the God wanted to kill my arrogance in the water itself. Despite my best efforts, my hands and legs had become weak. Not being possible to go for the fourth round, I had surrendered at the end of the three rounds. Cursing my misfortune, I got out of the water and walked towards the coach....

"Wah! Super! What a stamina! Marvelous!" said the coach shaking hands with me. That's not all, the selection committee members who were standing there, came to me and patted me on the back saying that I was excellent. I am standing before them with a loser's face and these persons are patting me. What is the matter? I was standing there without understanding anything of what they were saying. All those who were present there said Well done. I removed the swimming dress and changed to my original dress and followed them. We went through several passages, went to the third floor by lift and entered a room. The person asked me to sit there and after a while returned within two minutes with another officer, besides the lady who had spoken to me earlier. I was sitting there on a stool and staring at the walls.

That lady came inside and just said – "So, Mr. Basavaraj, I think you are selected". Coach continued "Well done my body, you swim quite well. Your stamina is also very good. You must change your swimming style slightly, that's all. We will give all such training. Don't worry". But my mind was worrying about the same thing. He asked, "what are you thinking"? "But I completed only three rounds, did not go for the fourth round at all. You have selected though I failed. That's what I don't understand" I told them. Laughing loudly, the coach said "Oh God, if you go for four rounds in the swimming pool, you will die. We consider only two rounds for the purpose of testing. Even the professional swimmers develop fear after the two rounds only. Whereas you have comfortably completed three rounds, which means – I think you have some special knowledge in swimming. We have still one or two rounds of formalities. Swimming while taking a load, swimming slowly like this. But looking at your swimming, we thought that you know swimming, but we need to provide you professional training. So, we did not do other tests. If you are interested, please sign here, if your father and mother have any objection, you should inform right now. Afterwards, you cannot run away on the pretext of remembering your parents. I told you as a precaution because some people come overenthusiastically and afterwards go away, that's why I told you this." At that point, I explained my life story briefly. That lady came near me and fondly brushed my head with her hands and said – "how much difficulties you have seen at such a young age. You have so much maturity. If you are selected here, you must quit the present job. If you leave the job, you will need a house to stay, isn't it? So, I will get an application form seeking permission to stay in the hostel. You please come tomorrow and sign the form – if you need the hostel, I will recommend and get it. Don't worry. You will earn some money during the training period. So, somehow you can manage. Once again, Let the Jesus bless you my son", wishing me, she shook my hand and returned. The coach came near me and asked whether I knew the way to go out. When I shook my head in the negative, he brought me for some distance and said go straight and take left there showing the building at a distance. I ran in one breath.

Shefali who was standing at a far away point, came running towards me and shook my hands "Congrats". How did you know, who told you? I asked. "Oho, you are a fool, you are really a fool. Who should tell? Can't I make out from your face which is glowing like a thousand-volt bulb? What happened, selected? She asked. "Yes" I said. Even her face was glowing like a thousand-volt bulb now. I admired her quality of finding her happiness in my happiness. Right, come let's go for a Vada-pav party she told. But one thing, I told her. She shook her as if to ask "What"? I feel like first informing Seena who is also part of my difficulties and happiness and then we will go for the party. Ok let's go, she started the scooter. The scooter started moving maneuvering the Bombay traffic.

"Your mother's pooja has yielded the result today. Somehow you have fulfilled your desire", Seena hugged me tightly. Our owner also came to know about this. He himself came to me and said "See my son, you have got a different job. But bringing a new person in your place will be difficult for me. But I will not be an obstacle to your dreams. Like you have been doing here, please work there also with the same loyalty. Wherever you are, God will support you. If you want to stay here for few days, I have no problem". I told him that I would be getting hostel accommodation. He blessed me by saying "that's good, best wishes". I touched his feet and showed my respect for him. I sat with Seena till two o'clock in the night, narrating my entire story. Listening to me he felt like sleeping, so went downstairs to his room. I continued to watch the stars and did not sleep even for a second.

*****

"Wow! Is this your house! It looks like a palace" saying so I glanced around the house. Yes, truly it was a palace. I asked her who are all there in the house. Coolly she said, "myself and my daddy". I asked her "What about your mother?". She just replied Hmm. She asked me to stay there so that she could park her scooter and close the gate. After parking the vehicle and closing the gate she came and opened the door. "Please come, you have come to our house for the first time", she said. The luxury inside was in no way inferior to any palace. Wow! Is it a house, a large hall where Sofas were placed on one side, a Buddha statue in front of the sofa, a large TV, walls full of mosaic tiles. A staircase connecting to the first floor. A large-sized kitchen, fridge, washing machine, for me it was like some dream.

Around six in the evening her few friends came. By seven in the evening, the party started. I was feeling bad due to the absence of Seena. Poor guy, it seems he wanted to come, but he was busy in preparations for the New Year. So, where will he have time for party? "By the by, this is my friend Basavaraju from Karnataka" Shefali introduced me to her friends. Is she hosting a party to celebrate my appointment in the military? Or does she just need a reason to have a party, and did I become that reason? I don't know. But I was deeply satisfied that the God has blessed me with a friend who finds happiness in my success and who smiles over my victory.

Though I was working in the bar from morning to night, I did not have the habit of drinking. So, I was holding some cooldrinks bottle in my hand. Shefali did not bother to even suggest me to drink. All that she told was "your wish, your choice, your freedom. I don't have the right to change it". Truly she was a unique person!

It was around nine thirty in the night, at last their liquor party reached the closing stage. Her friends greeted me once again and left. I told her that I will also leave as it was already nine thirty. "Where will you go in the night, stay here and go in the morning", she told. I will be feeling odd because I was alone with her in that massive house. Its okay I will leave, I will get the horse cart. Don't worry man, stay here. Don't be afraid of me, I will not rape you. Yes, her talks are like this only, very sharp like a knife's edge. She speaks straight forward without hiding anything, whether she is speaking to a male or female. I was a very shy type of person. I had grown in a different environment. Likewise, she has grown in her own environment. I decided to respect her words and stay there for the night.

"Do you stay alone always in this big house? Are you not afraid of it? Where is your father, he is not seen?" I asked her as if to break the silence. "Hmm, it is a big story. My dad is a famous civil engineer. Mother is a lecturer in Chemistry. When I was about twelve or thirteen years' old, they took divorce. Mother told the court that it was ok for her if I stay with dad. So, I stayed with my dad. Daddy is completely busy in his work, so he did not marry again. He said that he does not have that patience now. Anyhow, I was already a high school student. He wanted to perform my marriage in another six seven years, so that he completes his duties religiously. My daddy is famous in designing earthquake-resistant buildings. He is an expert in that field. So, he keeps touring different places regularly. This was said to be the reason for my mother to divorce daddy. Even now some dam construction work is going on. So, he is in Chandigarh. He will come in the next week. That's how I stay alone in this house. Earlier, one Punjabi auntie was coming to take care of household works and cooking. She was bringing her son also frequently. Somehow, I did not like some of his activities. So, I told daddy and removed them from service. Afterwards, we did not keep anybody else for these works. I prepare the breakfast in the morning and will finish the lunch in canteen. If there is any party in the night, I finish my dinner outside and come. Happy life", saying like this she walked towards the fridge to fetch a bottle of water.

"What happened to your marriage? How old are you now?", I asked her. "You fool! Don't you know that you should not ask a girl's age?". Yes, I had to eat my words for asking the wrong question. "Don't worry about my age. Marriage should have been over by now. But there was a breakup," she told. "May I ask what happened", I asked her. "Oh yes I am ready to tell. I also need a companion to narrate my story and forget my pain. I can talk about my breakup. But as it is you are a shy type of person. You should not be embarrassed by my open talk", she said. "It's ok, please tell, I have been telling about myself all these days and I never asked you anything about yourself, please tell me", I comforted her. "Okay, it's your funeral, what can I do, listen to me, Thousand Nine Hundred Thirty Third year....".

Stopping her midway, I told her "Hey, no need about all these preludes, say properly."

"Ha. Ok, I will narrate, listen to me", saying like this she started her story.

I was born in Punjab. At that time, daddy was working there only. Afterwards, I completed my school education in Karnataka and Rajasthan. By the time I entered the eighth standard, mother and father separated. I went into some depression at the time. Daddy got a new job during that time in Bombay. Daddy told me that he would stay alone for some time in Bombay and asked me to stay with his younger sister in Bhopal. "Anyway, its summer vacation now. I will bring school application in Bombay and admit you there, till then stay in Bhopal" he told me. Since she was daddy's sister, I thought I will also get a change and went there.

My aunt was taking care of me just like a mother, without giving any chance to me to remember my mother. She was a great cook also. Maava was working in some private company as accountant. It was a middle-class family. Aunt was also going to work at some garment factory. She would get up in the morning, prepare breakfast and lunch, pack her box and going for work. I would get up late, after brushing would take my bath, eat my breakfast, and sleep again. I was finding it difficult to pass the time. After a few days, aunt's son Pradeep came home. He was studying in a college in some place and was staying in the hostel. Since he was not allowed to stay in the hostel during summer vacation, he came home. In the first few days, he was not talking to me so much. It seems his mother had briefed him about me, divorce of mummy and daddy etc. Aunt, it seems, had told him that I was depressed a bit, so he should talk to me and make me comfortable. From that day, he started speaking to me occasionally. I was also happy that there was someone to talk to and spend my time.

Gradually, I became too much addicted to him. I like his style of talking, his hair style, his dresses jeans tea shirt – more than all these the kind of concern which he was showing towards me. Is it not natural at that age? I developed a sort of attraction towards him. Both of us started chatting for hours together. He was narrating his college stories to me, and his stories primarily focused on the girls in his college. I was also sharing my old story with him. I was explaining the lifestyle of people in Punjab, Karnataka, and Rajasthan.

One day, after finishing the breakfast, he was talking to me. It was a practice for me to complete my breakfast, lunch, close the kitchen and sleep for some time in the afternoons. After completing all the household works and after finishing our lunch, we were talking to each other. I told him that I would sleep for some half an hour and slept on the mat in the hall. Sitting next to me, he was watching some tv channel. Probably, I had not yet slipped into deep sleep, I was in a sleepy mood. Suddenly, I was thrilled. I was shocked in my sleep itself. I did not take long to realize what had happened, I continued to close my eyes and sleep. Yes, when I was in sleep, Pradeep had kissed me on my cheek. I did not know what to say. Should I scold him or should I tell aunt. But he is the only person I have, to talk and share my thoughts. If he gets angry with me and stops talking to me, what will I do? Moreover, aunt is taking care of me so affectionately, if I complain to her against her son, what would she think about me? Moreover, my entire body was brimming with my youth, and it found this thrill very soothing. I needed it more. So, I quietly slept as if I knew nothing. With a gap of just two minutes, that's all. He had given one more kiss as if to say buy one get one free. I experienced a sort of current passing through my body, I could not control myself, so I turned to the other side and slept.

Slowly he started to brush my head with his hand. Though some Hindi cinema was running on the TV, his whole concentration appeared to me on me only. The moment his soft finger touched my lips; I went through an explicable experience. My lips started trembling. The entire body started to shiver. Though I tried to control myself, I couldn't do so. Without knowing what to do, I continued to act as if I was sleeping. That was the only way left for me, I thought.

Whether he thought that I was sleeping or that I wouldn't oppose his act, He continued his act courageously. He forcefully pulled me towards him.

Even while acting as if I had fallen asleep, I turned on my back. Gradually he started to conquer me. He became more aggressive the moment I turned on my back. The virginity, which was just blossoming, and its structures had cast great effect on my body. When such a girl sleeps on her back, won't she look beautiful?

The feelings so natural to my age had turned me wild and I purposefully slept on my back. I wanted him to see the beauty of my body. I wanted him to become still more mad looking at my curvatures. The moment I slept on my back, He passionately kissed by lips with his lips. I also bit his lips roughly even while acting as if I was in sleep. I embraced him tightly. I had surrendered my youth, my feelings, and my entire beauty to him. He had conquered me completely. Our love story continued like this for many days. He was presenting me with a different type of gift every day. He was taking me outside for roaming without the knowledge of aunt. He was saying I love you hundred times every day. When he was saying I love you, I felt as if I was the happiest girl on this earth. He had become part of my life and I was feeling as if I could not live without him even for a day. I had dreamt of marrying him.

Afterwards, he started avoiding me. Then, I came to know from some people that he was a big playboy in his college. He seems to have had many girl friends in the college. I felt depressed about myself. I was happy all these days thinking that I had got a friend who would fill the place of father and mother. I felt that someone had burnt all my desires and turned them into ashes. By that time, father had shifted to this house in Bombay. I joined the college here only. Now, this house itself is my father, mother everything. I forgot him completely. I did not know that there was such a deep pain inside of Shefali who was presenting herself as the happiest person to the outside world. We were talking to each other throughout the night. I, as usual, started staring at the stars and went to sleep.

*****

5

Anyhow, my military life is starting from tomorrow. I am experiencing a sort of happiness and fervor. I bade goodbye to Seena once again. If I spend this night, yet another new life is starting for me. Hundreds of desires are sparkling in my eyes. I was sleeping on the terrace and speaking to Seena till one clock. When I look back at the path that I have traversed thus far, I couldn't believe myself. Leaving my place, coming to Bombay, getting a good job, a friend like Seena, an affectionate friend like Shefali, getting selected for the military job, hostel accommodation like icing on the cake – everything appeared to be the systematic plan of the Almighty! He has been with me all along and gracing me with some good developments. Especially I should be indebted to Shefali. She is not just a friend for me, but she is like a teacher to me. She had taught me all the speaking styles, body language, polished words to be used while conversing with different people, confidence required to defend ourselves etc. Wasn't she the one who personally took me to military and made me join there? How would this be possible without her? So, recalling the memories of my journey, I slipped into my sleep.

I took a horse cart at six thirty in the morning. After all what was my luggage – besides one or two pairs of dresses? Horse cart cannot enter the military camp. So, I got down near the gate and walked inside. Movement of people is very less in the morning time. Generally, there will be training session from six to nine in the morning. Everybody will be busy in that. After finishing the training, bath, and breakfast only people start moving out after ten – half past ten only. As informed earlier, hostel arrangement was made for me. Thus, I walked straight towards the hostel. After giving my details, I obtained the room key and entered the room.

The first day's work was quite enthusiastic. I was introduced to two of my roommates who were staying in the same room. I went around various facilities like hostel, dining hall, training place inside the military campus.

I even gave measurement for my uniform. After covering the one fourth of the campus, I went and spoke to madam. Had a talk with the coach for half an hour. Went to the dining hall, had my dinner, and returned to the room. Probably because I was tired of big round, I quickly slipped into a deep sleep. Got up five o'clock in the morning. Wow! How many days since I last saw the Sunrise! Was it not when I was in my place that I used to get up early in the morning and running towards the cattle shed?

After coming to Bombay and joining the work at the bar, everyday I was used to sleep late in the night and could not get up early in the morning. I was accustomed to a lazy life of getting up at eight or ten o'clock in the morning. After so many days, I am enjoying the breathtaking beauty of the rising Sun. Got up from the bed, freshened up and walked towards the training hall. The coach had already come there. With a lot of enthusiasm, I wished him namaste sir. The coach reciprocated with a good morning wish and told me that my uniform and swimming costumes had not yet come. They might come after three in the afternoon. Please come and meet me once in the evening. Go to the office, collect your dresses, and come tomorrow, take rest today, he told. Oho! Should I wait for one more day? With a disappointed face, I returned.

It was the third day of my hostel life – I had woken up at four thirty in the morning. I wore the uniform which I had collected just yesterday and stood before the mirror. I thought to myself "I am Basya, I bear several nicknames like stupid, ignorant, lazy, bad omen... etc., today standing in military uniform. Continuously staring at the mirror without moving my eyelids. I took about ten minutes to divert my look from the mirror. Am I not wearing the shoes for the first time? That's why I felt a bit of impatience. Doesn't matter, I will get adjusted to them after a few days. I packed the swimming suit in a bag and hung the bag to my shoulders, looked at the mirror once more and left for training. Since I had come little early, the coach had not yet come. He came in about fifteen minutes. I greeted him with a namaste, which he reciprocated and said 'Ha, ha namaste, come inside'. I followed him.

Though the training should have started at five in the morning, the coach came only at five thirty. The military training from five to seven in the morning is applicable for everybody. Afterwards, from department-related training sessions will be held from seven to nine. So, the coach took me directly to physical training field. I could hear the left-right voice from a distance. The coach introduced me to the instructor. I joined the rear row and started to follow the instructions. That training was scheduled for about two hours. My hands and legs started to pain already. After relaxing for five minutes, I reached the swimming academy as told by the coach. Immediately, I changed from uniform to swimming suit. Since I was already going to swimming pool, I did not feel odd about wear the swimming suit. As per coach's instruction, I got into the water. My hands and legs were paining because of two hours' physical training. But the moment I entered the water, pain completely disappeared. I got a new energy to swim. Since it was a first day, the coach did not teach me anything. All that he told me was "today is the first day of practice. So, whatever you know, whatever method you know, however you like you swim accordingly. I will observe your style, stroke and note down what all I will have to teach you." I answered him by saying "Yes Sir" and jumped into the water. Soon after getting into the water, I swam by my legs without using my hands and came out. I folded both the hands and swam. Without shaking the legs, I practiced swimming by using just the hands. Next, I experimented by floating on the water by lying on my back and bringing my hands and legs to straight position. I demonstrated all my skills in swimming to the coach including holding the breath and staying inside the water for a long time, throwing a heavy object into the water and diving inside to bring it out etc. He told "Not bad, enough come out". I came out and got into my uniform again. "Please go now, have breakfast and lunch, come here again at two in the afternoon" the coach instructed me. I saluted the coach by saying "yes Sir". I put the wet swimming suit in the bag and walked towards the hostel. I removed my uniform, had a bath, and wore my old shirt and pant. I went to the canteen, had my breakfast, and returned to my room. They had given me a special dryer to dry the swimming suit. I dried the swimming suit using that dryer and spread it in the sunshine at a place earmarked for the purpose. My room mates appeared to be sleeping already. Not willing to disturb them, I quietly came out of the room closing the door behind me.

I felt like taking one more round of the campus. So, I started to explore another side of the campus which I had not yet seen. I had not admired the military campus beauty even after three days. My first day was spent in completing the formalities, arranging my hostel room. Second day was also not different. I had spent most of the time in getting my uniform and swimming suits. By the time I could get my identity card, registering my name for food in the canteen, the day was over. Thus, I have got some time today only to go around the campus. After closing the door of my room quietly, I stepped out and started walking towards the east side of the hostel. Sprawling campus had enormous beauty to attract the inmates. Cool breeze, greenery all around, variety of flowers of different colors which I had not seen in my place, a small fountain in the middle of the park, three cranes in the water, no four of them. At the end of the park was a small lake adjacent to which few stone benches for sitting and enjoying the beauty. Butterflies flying over the flowers. If we walk straight from the park, there was a foot path. About one furlong from there, different structures specially designed for training. Next to them was a Kabaddi Court, a Small Volleyball Court to its right. Had I continued to walk, I could have walked the whole day. The campus was so vast! But I had to return, have lunch, and reach the swimming pool again. I decided to continue my campus round next time and return. The canteen was fully occupied by that time. Though I was tired of walking, I decided not to eat more as it may disturb my swimming and ate only two chapattis. I returned to my room, put the dried swimming suit into my bag and walked towards the swimming pool.

*****

Not one or two months, but complete three months are over. I did not have time to think of anything else other than my room, canteen food and swimming pool. I had met Shefali and Seena just two times in the last three months. My calculation of meeting them whenever I liked had gone wrong. None of us could go out of the campus without any valid reason and no outsiders could come inside – barring special occasions and exceptional reasons. Thus, of late, I am haunted by the memory of Shefali. I am craving to meet her at least once this week on some reason or the other. My training also is full of many surprise styles which I had never imagined. My coach is also teaching them to me with a lot of patience. I am spending half an hour extra in practicing them, but never tried to idle. Breaststroke, Back Stroke, Side Stroke, Butterfly Stroke, Front Crawl, Dog Pedal like this several swimming styles. Each one of them was quite exciting than the other and each one of them was unique. A person who was swimming in the village pond, has become a swimmer and has learnt to speak English and Hindi.

*****

At last, that much awaited day has arrived. The first stage of my training had completed. There was a short break of three days for the training. So, I took the permission of my coach and went out for two days. First, I reached the bar which provided me the precious shelter when I landed in Bombay. To my misfortune, Seena had gone to his native place for fifteen days. Had he not told that he would not go to his village? Then, where else did he go? Has he really gone to his village? Thinking like this, I walked towards Shefali's house.

"Wow, at least you are there", saying like this I entered her house. She did not appear to be so enthusiastic to see me after so many days. "Why are you so dull, what is the matter"? I asked her. "Nothing", she replied. I was very happy indeed to meet her after many days. Though she appeared to have lost in her own world, gradually she regained her original rhythm. We spoke to our heart's content. I reported my three months' experience of military life.

She was also chatting continuously covering her daily routine, new movie, cricket and so on. It was getting dark. That was the time when mosquitoes would enter the house. She asked me to wait a minute, went and closed the windows as well as the door, lighted the mosquito coil. No sooner than she returned, continued her talks. Only for two minutes, she had taken some break. Her talks were like the sea viewed from the India Gate in Bombay; it was infinite. What special? I asked her. She asked me to wait and went inside again. I was watching some English movie being played on the television.

*****

6

Wow! What a waterfall! Those who are looking at it, are sure to miss their breath for a while. The force of the water was like the arrow from the bows of Arjuna. The roaring sound of waterfalls may even silence the elephant's trumpet! That enormous sound was something like the effect of thousands of lightnings striking at once. People of that place, it appears, had not seen the falls roaring like that anytime in the past. Yes. The water released from a dam situated at a far away distance has multiplied the force of the falls. That pair, however, seems to be unaware of the increasing discharge of water from the reservoir. They are engrossed at the peak of their love making.

He is a musician, no parallel to his talent in the entire state. He had become popular not only in his motherland but also all over the world. He had sacrificed his life to set aside the traditional formulae and experiment his own new techniques. What kind of difficulties he has gone through to achieve something in the field of music? He was on the verge of begging even for one meal. That doesn't mean that he was very poor. The king himself had admired him for being the unconquered champion in fencing. Tom was his own father. This John was the only son of Tom. Father aspired to make his son a supreme soldier just like him. He has his own reason for this. During the previous war, he had lost one of his hands. Thus, he had to run his family from the monthly pension sanctioned by the King. A small family comprising of himself, wife, and a son. Thus, the honorarium-monthly pension given by royal family, enough property left behind by the elders were helping to lead a comfortable life. But his concern was bravery with which he had beheaded hundreds of enemy soldiers in the battlefield and earned the title 'maha shoor' from the king himself, and he knew that there was no count of enemy soldiers who were coming forward to surrender before the king, owing to his fear. It is impossible for such a person to sit at home and wait for the monthly pension sanctioned by the king. Tom had even thought of committing suicide on several occasions.

But for generations his family had dedicated itself to the service of royal family. When such is the case, it is unethical to even think of dying without the order of the king. So, Tom gave up the idea of dying and started to teach all the skills to his son so as to make him a great soldier and present him before the king. As they say 'man proposes, God disposes', Jack was thinking otherwise. Jack was staying away from war, violence etc. He had become depressed as he knew that his father lost his hand because of the war. He had developed an inexplicable hatred for war and violence. Tom consequently developed contempt towards his son for belying his ambitions. But his love for Jack had remained the same. A ray of hope was still alive in him thinking that his son will fulfill his dream one day or the other. But Tom received a new which shattered all his dreams. He started developing hatred towards his son for ruining his desires. The hatred feeling forced him to throw his son out of his house. Though Jack was struggling to get even the food, and everybody sympathized with him, nobody came forward to help him. They were afraid of inviting the wrath of Tom who hated Jack. All said and done, Tom was a right hand to the king, and they were afraid of possibly inviting king's anger by trying to help Jack. Thus, they were giving Jack little food for his survival, except this they were not helping him in any other way. If Jack was to die of starvation, will not bring bad name to the king also? Thus, the king would not be angry if food was given in alms. He would be quiet as if he has not seen anything. With this belief only Jack was getting food from people and was surviving. Tom on the other hand was feeling sad over the misery of his son. Whenever he was reminded of the cruel treatment meted out to his son, Tom was becoming wild. He never thought that this itself will take a heavy toll on him one day. And it did! It took the life of Tom and made Jack an orphan. The root cause of making Jack an orphan and a beggar was none other than Jack's

....

"Passion for Music".

*****

Jack's hatred and enmity for his father multiplied after the latter threw him out of the house. Afterall, what was my mistake? If father likes to fight in battles, why should I become a soldier? Though the rule mandates King's son to become a King, it does not bind a soldier's son to become a soldier or a sculptor's son to become a sculptor. If the King's son does not succeed his father, the matter may become a laughingstock in public. But the soldier's son does not have such a binding. Why can's a businessman's son become a painter? Why can't a thief's son become a dancer? Though the profession may come by inheritance, hobby can be chosen according to one's choice, isn't it? I will ensure that the same king who was admiring his father will admire me also for being a greater musician and will see that he felicitates me for being an expert. Though the king was admiring my father, his position was limited to standing before the king hands folded. On the other hand, a sculptor, musician, vidooshak, poet, comedian, magician will bear the title of experts and will be sitting in front of the king. The king appreciates the poets, artistes as the gems of his kingdom and he does not say so about the soldiers. Thus, it is prudent to choose music which brings a lot of mental peace to war which is bound to mentally disturb you, besides unleashing enormous amount of violence. The urge to become one of those gems in the kingdom motivated Jack against committing suicide and accomplish the art of music even at the cost of begging. Jack was never an idling person. He was roaming around the places and meeting the great personalities. He was learning a week's lesson in just a day and a day's lesson in just a minute! He had toured hundreds of places, met scores of experts, and enriched his reservoir of music knowledge. Gradually the king came to know of his urge for learning. The king was feeling heart of heart very happy about the accomplishment of Tom's son. How would the king know that this knowledge of Jack will one day sink him completely?

*****

"Hi! My name is Catherine. I am an orphan as I don't have my parents. I live in the church. The church is my home! Your music has mesmerized me very deeply. I have become your fan. I am observing since many days that you come here every morning, listen to the chirping of the birds and sing along with them. That's how I wanted to meet you once, so I came here. Let's catch up again, bye" saying so she had disappeared in just two minutes. For Jack, who was just attaining his youth, the talks of Catherine were like drinking nectar. Not just her talks, but also her beauty. She was an apsara. Jack was beaming with happiness because there was at least one person who admired his music. As time passed by, Jack was becoming famous all over the state. The king himself had listened to his music a couple of times while touring. Every marriage and other functions would not go without Jack's concert. As the popularity of Jack kept on increasing, the love between Jack and Catherine also started becoming that much intense. Both were meeting atop the rock near the water falls once a week. Catherine was enjoying the singing of Jack blended with the sounds of the water falls unmindful of everything and everyone around her. How could Catherine or Jack realize that such a grave tragedy would strike even while listening to the music. The overflowing water from the falls had covered the tip from all four directions. It was impossible to swim against the force of the water and reach the shore. Death was assured even if they swam or stayed there. Jack is wondering how did so much water enter all at once even when there was no rain. How to escape from there? How to rescue Catherine? Five minutes would suffice for the gushing water to swallow them. Even if they started swimming right now, it is not possible to reach the shore in five minutes. "I am sorry Jack", saying this Catherine embraced Jack rightly. The force of her tears was far greater than that of the water flowing towards the falls. She held me tightly and said "I am sorry Jack. Because of me you had to lose your life. I am responsible for this, please forgive me." Jack looked at her shockingly. Kissed her passionately and said – "mad of you. They would have probably opened the gates of the falls. That's how water flow has increased. How can you be responsible for this!" They were already in the water to their knee length. Anyway, it is impossible to escape now. Hence, they decided to die together. They have forgotten everything while kissing each other passionately. Controlling her sobbing, Catherine said.

"I am sorry Jack. Please forgive me. One lie that I uttered today is taking your life".

"A lie? What is that?" asked Jack. He was embracing Catherine resisting the water which had raised to their chest level. "Yes. What you told may be correct. The king, who could not accept our love, would have ordered the opening of dam gates. It may be impossible for them to accept our love. So, please forgive me. By the way, do you know what is the lie that I told you? Listen to me. Fearing that you may not accept my love, if you know who really, I am, I suppressed the fact and told you that I was an orphan. I am sorry" she said holding the water which had come up to the neck level.

Jack looked at her more surprisingly, and in a shell shock. He controlled the water which had raised above the neck level and asked her "What has the king got to do with our love? What is his relationship with our love? I don't understand anything". Catherine, with great difficulty resisted the water which was to her ears' level by now and told – "I am not an orphan. I am the princess of this kingdom. You asked what is the relationship between us and the king, isn't it? Listen. He is my father! Please forgive me! Telling that I was an orphan might be a lie, but my love is not. I love you Jack" saying so she embraced Jack tightly. The next moment water had completely swallowed both.

*****

"What Sir? You seem to have lost in some world. Please return to our world" I was momentarily shocked by the words of Shefali. "Oh! What kind of love she was in" I murmured? "Whose love I say?" I did not have an answer to Shefali's question. I could not utter a word. How infinite was the love of Catherine who suppressed the fact that she was a princess and like to Jack that she was an orphan! Though the movie was over long back, its impact on my mind could not end easily, I am not able to forget it. Even if I close my eyes, the pictures of Jack and Catherine are haunting me. "Hello" Shefali forcefully shook me and made me return to reality. I explained her "Nothing, some English movie was coming on TV. I was intensely viewing it. The heroin of the movie loves the hero so much that she dies with him". "Yes, yes. You understand the love story that comes on TV, but you don't realize the love story in real life," she teased me. I asked her "what is the real love story?" "Nothing, come I will tell you when the time comes" smiled and took me to the verandah. "You said that you would return quickly and went inside. Where were you so long?" "Oh! I met you after a long time, isn't it? So let us celebrate. I was preparing for the party. Come let us have a drink", she told. Wow! In the shortest time available, she has prepared two three types of dishes. Not sure whether she cooked or got them from the hotel. There were two wine bottle glass and some two bottles of cool drinks on the table. "Sorry Shefali! Though I was working in the bar, I don't have the habit of drinking" I told her. She giggled and said "Hello Sir, I also know it. That wine is for me. The cool drinks bottles which are there at a corner of the table are meant for you. "What is that, suddenly you have opted for the wine"? I asked her. "Oho, do you remember my brand also? Nothing... just like that.... Of late, I am not consuming anything other than wine. That too home-made wine. Got it from Pondicherry. I had not touched it for many days. Today you have come, so... let us celebrate, cheers" she said. Our party started.

There was a complete silence between the two of us. No talking whatsoever. They say that the deep silence bears enormous meaning than thousand words. Yes! The human being should invent himself. Instead of undertaking voyage to other planets, he should delve deep into himself and instead of craving to the see the God, should try to contact his soul. One should possess vast knowledge but remain as if he does not know anything. He should be able to listen to his heartbeat even amid crowd in the fair, bells of the temple, thunders and lightnings. Yes! All of us, in

fact, should slip into this condition at least once. Should be like a dumb, alone, quiet. One should explore his inner self and try to find out who am I? When the body is awake, one should try to push the consciousness to sleepiness. The body and mind should be allowed to float freely in the blue sky just like the flying birds. Soul should be carried from loneliness to seclude; mind should be carried from pollution to purity. With blissful state of mind, sea of calmness should be swum, and shore should be reached. Like this, every human being should re-invent himself, that too by himself. Presently, I and Shefali are experiencing that condition.

Shefali while thinking about her future...

Me forgetting my past...

*****

"I love you da" her words pierced through the silence. On the one side, I was going through the unbearable pain of someone pulling me towards them and on the other, inexplicable happiness of God himself appearing before me. I don't know what was happening to me in contradicting situations of pain and happiness. "I am telling you again that I love you" I regained my consciousness to the repeated words of Shefali. We were into some half an hour after the party commenced and it was Shefali who broke the silence with just one sentence "I love you da" ...

"Hello, I told you only; I am repeating again. I love you man" within two minutes I was back to normal. "Do you think I am talking in intoxicated condition? Don't you know my drinking capacity? Yes, I say. I am talking just normally, listen to me – You are an orphan without anybody, anything. I am an orphan even while having everything. In a sense both of us orphans. Just for name's sake I have mommy and daddy. No love, no affection. You know about my friends. If I spend money and host a party, there will be with me. Otherwise, they will not bother whether I am dead or alive. Mine is a sort of lonely life. The only person who talks to me without any selfish motive, the only person who loves me from the bottom of his heart is you. Only you and no one else. Were you not talking about Catherine in that movie? I have ten times more love on you. I don't know what you have or what you don't have. But you have the mind of a child, you don't know have a crooked mind. That's enough for me. That's what I liked of you. I wanted to confide this matter with you earlier itself but was afraid to do so fearing that you may distance yourself from me. That's why I was controlling my feelings till now. I may become the root cause of ruining your dream of joining the military. So, I had controlled myself with great difficult by not disclosing this to you. I had not seen you for two-three months; I was feeling contented by speaking to you at least. Today, when I saw you after a long time, I could not resist myself from disclosing my mind to you. Now, I am relaxed. I feel like living with you till my last breath. Please don't say no. Without any shame, I am proposing to you. I am finding it extremely difficult to live without you, please try to understand" saying like this she embraced me. I was in a state of confusion, not able to understand anything. Without my knowledge, my hands embraced her. "I love you too Shefali" the words came out of me automatically. The scene of Jack and Catherine holding each other was repeating again and again, not on TV screen, but in my eyes.

Would the love between Basya and Shefali also be a tragedy like that of Jack and Catherine? Who knows?

*****

"Basya and Shefali who are at opposite corners of Karnataka and Bombay have come together in Bombay, isn't it so surprising?" Shefali said. "Yes surprising! At the same time a mystery also. The destiny has brought me from somewhere and imprisoned me in the cage of love", I to her. We don't know how long we had been talking like this. We ate some two rotis and Jeera Rice and continued our talk. I told her "Okay, its already late, I will take leave of you". "Where to" she asked. To the hostel, before completing I realized that it was not possible to reach the hostel at this hour. Moreover, I had taken permission to go out for three days. So, where will I go in the midnight? What about going to the bar where I was working earlier? But Seena is not there. As I was thinking, she asked "Hello, what are you think about?". "I am thinking where to sleep", I told her. You sleep here with me, she told which I found to be little awkward. She continued "Why? Should you not sleep here? Is this not your house?" 'Not like that, it does not look nice if only we two are here", I expressed my reservation. "Oh, it is like that. I believe you; I know that you are a good boy" she expressed confidence in me. "I also know that. My fear is not that. I don't have faith in you. My fear is what if something happens to me", I teasingly told her. Both of us laughed to our heart's content. Shefali came near me, wrapped her both the hands around my neck and told – "Let me tell you something. Both of us are lovers. Though we expressed our love to each other a few moments ago, the love between the two of us blossomed long back. Jack and Catherine also were lovers only, they did not marry. That is for the outer world. They were couple in their hearts and minds. Mental marriage had taken place already. When it comes to marriage, I don't have faith in marriage, thali etc. How is that they are strangers a moment before tying the thali and become husband and wife immediately? In the worldly tradition, thali, marriage is just a media. Just a symbolic representation. If they can be accepted as husband and wife immediately after tying the thali, why two hearts who have accepted each other as husband and wife cannot be recognized like that? Thali and marriage are a state of mind. Have not you heard of stories involving marriages of couple like Dushyantha and Shakunthale? Why cannot we think ours as a Gandharva marriage? Look – I am a very open-minded person. You also know that. I have told you everything about me starting my boy friend to everything else. I have not hidden anything from you. I also don't like you hiding anything from me. Just because I am forcing you or because of some ulterior motive, you should not love me. If so, please tell the truth now itself. I don't need your love born out of compulsion. I will remain like this for the rest of my life. Whether you believe it or not, my marriage is already over. I have become your wife the moment you accepted my love. If you are keen to observe the symbolic representation of tying the thali, please get the cross tied to that photo of Jesus and tie it to me. You may be happy then at least. Why should we worry about the customs of this society which made you wonder on the streets and made me feel like an orphan even with everything? Even if you were to die of hunger on the streets of Bombay, this society would not have come to your rescue. They would have treated your dead body as that of an orphan and thrown into the Corporation lorry. If you die while serving the military, the same society will admire you as a martyr. So, when our marriage is already over, why should we bother about the customs of this society? It is your will and wish! Tie the Cross, I have not objection", she told him.

"Whether we like it or not, since we are living in a society, we should observe certain customs. For example, tomorrow you cannot go to the military office and change my marital status as married, they will ask for the evidence. Either a photograph of the marriage or marriage certificate from the registrar should be shown. But you may face problem in your current job. So, just to silence the society, let us go to some temple or registrar's office. Remember – its only for the outside world. We are already husband and wife. Okay? Come! When my daddy comes next time, I will tell this to him also. You may officially tie the thali in front of him. Let that also be completed" saying so she smiled and went inside.

Shefali's talks are like that only, straight forward. Her mind also is like that! Totally transparent. Her thoughts too were totally clean. I looked up towards the photo of Jesus, such a smiling face! Next to him was Sai Baba, flanked by Lord Krishna preaching Bhagavad-Gita. I had really surrendered to Shefali's thought process, lifestyle. Whatever she told was true, isn't it? As is our mind, so is Lord for us. Our talks-life will be that much purer as our mind would be. Is it not sufficient to invoke God? Why do we need these scenes of marriage, thali etc." With these thoughts I walked inside.

Shefali is blissfully lying on the bed after venting out all her pent-up feelings. I am lying with the confusion thinking whether this was a dream or a reality. I found a new meaning to my life on this day. Shefali is mine. Shefali is mine from today. She is mine forever. When I did not know for whom, I should live, she has come as an answer in my life. I will leave for her. Her dream is my dream. I will guard her in such a way that she never sheds tears in life. Even at the cost of my life. "Hello, my dear husband" aren't you getting sleep? She asked me. "No" I said. "I know. Now it will come, come" she pulled me towards her and embraced me tightly. I was imprisoned in her shoulders.

Like never before, Shefali is looking very beautiful. It is true that she is not supremely beautiful, but she is beautiful. But she is looking far more beautiful in the blue colored night bulb. Her contented face has enhanced her beauty. Her beauty is multiplied by the blue light. Wasn't it the thin purple color gown which she was wearing for the party? What a contrast between her skin color and the light purple gown? Wow! She is in no way second to any apsara. Light had fallen on the displaced dress is displaying her body curves beautifully in the blue light... I am going mad looking at her body structure. Vital parts of a female body which must be in their right proportion are richly standing out at the right places. Matching her breathing, her body is heaving up and down, accentuating her beauty hundred times! Her silky hairs are flying to the cool breeze of the fan and are kissing her cheeks. The pink-colored lip stick is smiling on her lips. Her diamond-studded earrings, rainbow-like eyebrows, nose-stud decorating her nose enhanced her beauty just like the nature just drenched in the rain. I am not the candle not to melt in her warm embrace. Can I divert my sight from the edge of her thin gown? In her sleepiness, she is further tightening her embrace. With that, my feelings too.

I pulled her towards me and passionately kissed her. The aroma of her shampoo-washed hair is making me mad. Her body contact with my body is enraging me sensually. My hands, without my knowledge, are roaming all over her body. Both of us are totally in the grip of sensuality as if we are hit by the arrows of Madana. In short, we are not married, but we have. This is not our first night; but it is the first night.

*****

Three days had passed just like that. I had become more enthusiastic about myself, my wife, my house, my family. Shefali is now just like my wife. She had served me with abundant love and affection in just three days, which a wife does to her husband in her lifetime. Entire day was full of eating, talking, happiness, anger, romance. I was bathed in a balanced mix of everything of these elements. Thus, I did not know how the three days had passed by. Finally, my leave period was coming to an end, and it was time to take leave of Shefali and continue with the hostel life. Not sure when would I be able to see Shefali next. Shefali bade goodbye to me with tears in her eyes. My autorickshaw moved towards the military campus.

*****

"We have not seen such an amazing swimmer. Instead of keeping him in the military campus, if we send him for the Olympics, our country is sure to win a gold", said the trainer. I was focusing on just the training for the next two and a half months. The water should feel contented by seeing my swimming because I was spending so much time in the water. I was forgetting the world around me while swimming. I was swimming at every available opportunity in the morning, evening, after lunch without feeling bored. Though my training was limited to only five hours a day, I used to spend ten to twelve hours in the water. I was learning all the styles and tricks taught by the trainer. I was, in fact, becoming his teacher with respect to some strokes. The telephone booth located at the end of the campus had kept the bondage between me and Shefali intact. We were chatting with each other every evening. There was no limit to her happiness on listening to my progress in training. Just one month's training was left, that's all. Afterwards, I would also become a soldier. Shefali jubilated on hearing this from me. She said that she had already explained her father about us. Though her father did not agree initially, she somehow convinced him and got his green signal for our marriage. I was feeling the thrill of even thinking that myself and Shefali are getting married and setting up our own family soon after completing my training in the next one or one and a half months' time. We don't know for how many times both of us would say "I love you" to each other every day. More than ever before, I was very happy today. That one statement of Shefali has made me feel as if I was on cloud nine. I feel the urge to meet her once. But these fifteen days of final round of training her very strict. I cannot go anywhere, or no one can meet me. It does not mean that I was barred from meeting anybody – it was the self-imposed restriction to hold our concentration till the end, it was not the restriction imposed by the military rule book. Anyway, I could meet her everyday on completion of these fifteen days of training. I consoled myself that I should somehow control myself for fifteen days. Still, I am very keen to see her face once. I feel like listening to those golden words repeatedly what she told me this evening.

The words which painted vibrant colors to the wings of my feelings were – "Congrats, you are becoming a father I say".

*****

"Enough Basya! Get up. How much do you drink? Except spoiling your health by drinking so much, you are not going to achieve anything. Get up". I did not listen to the words of Seena at all. I am fed up with this life itself. If snatching from me was inevitable, why was it given to me at all? Did I ask the God to give me her love? No. I was living somewhere, somehow; she came like a thunder and disappeared like a thunder. She says she feels nauseating to see my face. What sin did I commit? How many colorful statements she had made? 'Let us get married soon after your training gets over. We will have a small house for ourselves in which you, me and our cute child will be there. I will love you much more than Catherine.' Just last month she had announced that I was becoming a father. Not sure whether it was true or not. Would she have enjoyed playing with my feelings? It is told that some people have this kind of vicarious mental sickness. During our training, one Colonel had explained that there were a large number of such mental patients in the society. Just to find pleasure in others' pain, they seem to carryout criminal activities. One thing is clear – she is also some type of vicarious mental patient. Otherwise, why she had to talk of marriage, setting up our home and other things? Everything an utter lie! Her father had agreed for our marriage, who knows? While speaking to me over phone, she had announced that I was becoming father and she was in to her third month. What is the proof of this? That was also told over phone. It could possibly be a series of lies just to instigate my feelings. Perhaps she needed just the physical pleasure from me. Was not she roaming around with boy friends in the name of parties? Maybe she was bored of those boyfriends, and she needed a new one and found that in me. What kind of life I am going through? I should have come under the train that day itself. As they say, a sinner has hundred years. I am like that. That's why I fell into her trap. Let her go do dogs. I kept on cursing her. "Hey Basya, cool down and tell me what happened. Somewhere, something has gone wrong! Shefali is not a bad girl. I will go and talk to her" Seena told me.

"Do you want to talk to that dirty girl? If you allow, she will also trap you. She is like that; she is not a good girl".

"Okay, she is a bad girl. Please explain what exactly happened," Seena told me. Controlling my sobbing, I started narrating whatever happened since yesterday morning.

"I am having one week holiday since the day before yesterday. I have completed my training period, you know. So, I could take a week's leave and go around. All my friends went to their respective places. Yesterday morning, I took an auto and went to Shefali's house. I had not disclosed about my holiday just to give her a surprise. Moreover, it was already ten fifteen days since she spoke to me over phone the last time. Whenever I dialed her number, it was ringing but nobody was answering. I did not know whether she had gone out of station, or whether there was any emergency, or even I did not know whether she was in Bombay at all. I expected her to rejoice over seeing me, embrace me shyly with my child inside her. So, I went straight to her house yesterday morning. The moment she saw me, she became pale. She did not speak to me or even did not give a smile. She did not even call me inside. I felt a bit disappointed. Equally surprised too. She often gets angry with me and imitates this type of anger with me. I thought that day also she was acting like that. How are you Shefali? My training period is over and no more hostel life. I have one week holiday. Next Monday only I will attend the duty. So, I thought of seeing you, here I am. How is my son? Son or Daughter? What does he say? Was he enquiring about me? How are you? We will go tomorrow itself and find a house for rent. From tomorrow, both of us will live in our house, I am very happy today. "I love you Shefali", saying this I embraced her. "Leave me alone please! I feel irritated. Why did you come here? Who asked you to come? With whose permission did you come? Please go away?" she said. Assuming that she wants to pester me more, so that I pet her in the process, I spoke to her in a very cute manner "Oho, what happened to my baby? Are you angry? Even in your anger, how beautiful you look? My doll is so sweet". "Please leave me alone" she screamed at the top of her voice. A clear hatred was seen about me. I did not find an iota of love in her behavior. Despite that, I went near her and calmly asked "What happened Shefali, are you angry? What mistake did I commit? If you tell me, I will correct myself" and embraced her. She released herself from my clutches and slapped me on my face. Without my knowledge, I started crying. "You idiot! Don't you understand what I am telling you? You have not committed any mistake. I don't want to see your face. Don't you appear in front of me ever again. If you try to speak to me, I will die. This is the last meet between the two of us. Don't ask for the reasons. You know about me if you come again to see me that's all. I am telling you clearly once again, please listen carefully "I hate you" I don't want you. Please go away. If you try to talk to me again, you will see my dead body. Now get out of my house", saying this she slammed the door on my face.

Listening to my narration, Seena started laughing loudly. I became still wild looking at his laughter. I felt like slapping him. Seena said "Oh, that's all! I thought the world has doomed". Without understanding, I simply looked at him. Seena continued "Like she told you, you are really an idiot. About fifteen twenty days back, you had told me that you had not received phone call from Shefali and asked me to go to her house and enquire about her, isn't it? Please recall. I had told you that these girls are like that only. During their pregnancy their mood swings rapidly. They suddenly become dull, suddenly they become active, get angry, suddenly they become so affectionate. Did I not tell you?" "Yes" "That's not all, please listen – their feelings, their thoughts keep varying. Perhaps she would have fought with her father over the marriage issue. Or someone close to her would be in some difficulty. She would have shown her anger towards someone else on you. Except you, who else is there for you? She will call you in a day or two, don't worry", he said. "I know Shefali very well, I am not that incapable to not find out her real anger".

Seen replied "Yes, I agree. You are the great superman. Okay? I will tell you another thing, please listen"

"I hate you";
"I cannot withstand you";
"You are my life";
"I love you more than my life";
"I will leave my father and mother for your sake";
"Let us be together like this till the last";
"I don't need your riches – you are enough for me";
"I don't have the strength to live without you";
"If you say no, I will die";
"You will get a better girl than me"; "Please forget me";
"Please leave me alone"; "Ours is the bondage of seven births"

These are all the common dialogues of the girls I say. They should be delivering such dialogues every now and then. If a girl does not utter these words in front of her boyfriend, he should presume that there was some problem. "Shefali told you that she does not want to see your face and asked you to go away, isn't it? So, she is normal. After a few days, she will be all right. Please remember this secret always" Seena laughed saying these words.

*****

"See Srinivas, I am a very matured woman. My age is not to behave in a childish manner. I don't need him, that's all. I don't want to live with him. Very simple. I don't understand why you are making this a big issue. Please go and tell him that I don't need him". Listening to these curt words of Shefali, Seena was also shocked. But can he keep quiet. He had come here assuring Basya that he will speak to Shefali and solve the problem. He told her "All that is okay Shefali. But just a few days back you had told that you cannot live without him, what happened to that love today? If there is any misunderstanding, please let me know. I will talk to him". "Nothing like that. Even if it is there, I cannot share my feelings with a third person", Shefali's words hit Seena like an arrow. "All right don't share it with me. At least, why don't you sit with your husband and discuss? Poor guy, he is suffering like a fish out of the water. He does not know anything except chanting your name. Like him, his love is also pure. At least, for the sake of humanitarian consideration, why don't you sit and discuss with him for some five minutes? He is here only, I will call him inside, both of you should speak openly, please" pleaded Seena. "I don't need your preaching. Don't teach me about humanitarian values. You are forcing me repeatedly even after I told you that I don't want to discuss further. You should learn the lesson of humanitarian values. Finally, I am telling, I don't want to talk to anyone. Just get out". "Okay madam, I will go. But please tell me one thing. Is the news of you becoming mother to his child is true or false?". Now, it was her turn to feel the shock. Shefali thought that this argument would not end anytime soon unless and until she attacks the ego of Seena. "It is none of your concern. It is between me and my husband. This is a secret between husband and wife. Why do you want to discuss such things? Are you not ashamed of asking personal matters of others? Is this the culture your parents have taught you?" Shefali had succeeded in her plan. It had hit the right place. Seena was hurt because she had blamed his parents. "Okay madam! I have heard a lot about arrogant people. I came here as a well-wisher. There is no personal gain or loss in this matter. You needed someone to fulfill your urge and my friend walked into your trap. He told bye to her and got up to leave. She held his hand said, "one small request". 'What is that"?, he asked. "Please tell him not to show his dirty face ever again". Silently cursing her for the arrogance, Seena left the place.

Both don't know that I was listening to their discussion hiding behind the tree.

*****

My eyes are completely dried of crying. I am not feeling hungry at all. If not having strength in the body is one worry, the other worry is that Seena had to listen to her abuses because of me. I don't have the courage to show my face to Seena. He was everything to me – a friend, relative, teacher. But, had to bow is head in front of a girl, all because of me. Seena was like my godfather who was responsible for whatever I have got today. So to say, he was the one who took me to the swimming pool, otherwise how could I get the opportunity to join the military? In return, I have not given him anything, am I not a selfish fellow? This is the greatest gift I have given to Seena – suffering humiliation at the hands of Shefali, just for my sake. I was lost in my thoughts. "Look Basya, I know what you are thinking about", saying so he came near me. "You are disturbed because she scolded me, isn't it? She did it so deliberately. She appeared to be feeling disturbed over my repeated pleas on your behalf. It was just her preplan to silence me and she does not have any hatred towards me. Let me tell you this, her confidence in me would have multiplied after observing me tolerating all her humiliation. One thing is confirmed. She does not really like you, but she is not in a position to tell the reason. So, she feels hurt if we go on digging her mind. The only we she had to escape from this discussion was to scold me, because she knew that I did not have any other topic to discuss with her other than yours. So, she has scolded me only to silence me and not heart of heart. I am not worried at all."

Seena's personality to bear so much insult for the sake of his friend made me even smaller in front of him. My love for Shefali had burst like a balloon. Can I afford to lose Seena for the sake of a selfish and arrogant Shefali? Seena made me get up – "Already it is four days since you came to me. You had not drunk alcohol ever before, but in these four days how much a drunkard you have become. You have not eaten properly. Being a human being should you not eat something? There is no use in thinking about her only. We will go out tomorrow, now have some food". I told him "I am not hungry, leave me alone just today" and slept on the mat. "Okay, you be to yourself today, you will also get some consolation. But don't keep on worrying too much. Sleep properly. Customers will be waiting, bye take rest" Seena left.

*****

"What? You keep on talking of committing suicide? Is it a child's play? Stupid fellow", the moment I heard Seena shouting at me, I lost all my courage. I did not have the strength to answer him back. I would have perhaps given a fitting reply to my father if he was in Seena's position, but to Seena I could not answer back. I am afraid of even looking at him face to face. "What else can I do? She left me, all of them have cheated me. My anger is not at Shefali, but on the God who has brought me to earth to lead this kind of miserable life. I don't need this misery, I will die. What is the use of living such a life? To tell the truth, I have already died, only my body is alive. Perhaps my mother is eager to meet me, that's why she is giving all these difficulties to me. She knows I will die unable to bear this misery and join her in the heaven. Please don't stop me" I told him unmindful of my tears.

"Just because that mad girl has spoken like this, will you commit suicide? Last time also you had tried to jump in front of a train. Are you repeating the same today? Have not you learnt a lesson from your experience thus far? Forget about her. Please live for your sake. You had told me that you had not given me anything. Today I am asking you something. Stop thinking about suicide in any situation. You lead a successful life which should envy her who has abandoned you. She should shed tears just as you are doing now. Not just Shefali, even your aunt who threw you out of the house. You should pay her back with interest. Please realize that you are not the only one who is suffering in the world, there are many persons like you. Do you think all of them commit suicide? Remember, you are not the same Basya anymore, you are a soldier who carries enormous responsibility of saving a large number of people who are in problem. Forget her and start thinking about your duties. Think and act in such a way that she comes to us and expresses regret over her conduct. Instead of dying under a moving train, sacrifice your life in the battlefield. That death will have a purpose and meaning. Your mother will be happy over your achievement. Decide yourself whether you will live to fulfill the dream of your mother or die because of the girl who ditched you".

Seena's talks hit me like hundred lashes. Why was I wasting my time and energy on love, marriage, family etc., instead of focusing on the duty which

I had lovingly chosen. I will live and prove that I can live without her. She told me not to show my face to her. I will make her come to me and regret her utterance. I will not even dream of her. Now onwards, she will be my life-long enemy". "Super, come let us go. One week's leave is over, your work starts from tomorrow, isn't it? Let us go" he said.

Just like Arjuna followed Lord Krishna, I went behind Seena.

*****

7

Snow-clad mountain range all around. Which is the mountain? Which is the earth? Which is the cloud? Could not make out anything. Wonderful creation of God was such that its beauty neither can be explained nor the truth behind His creation be understood. Infinite view of the white mountains. Had not Lord Shiva himself made Himalaya as his home? The white color was multiple times whiter than the cow milk, jasmine flower, and the clean cotton. Himalaya – appearing to be decorated with Rangoli and jasmine flowers; Himalaya – the auspicious birthplace for the holy Ganga. Himalaya – hallowed by the footprints of hundreds of saints who did relentless meditation which had the enormous power to conquer the whole world! Breathtaking beauty of Himalaya – Not able to make out whether the mountain was in the snow or snow was on the mountain! Clean water flowing through the mountain – not sure whether they were springs, rivers, lakes. One thing is true. If there was a competition between nectar consumed by Gods and Pure Water at the Himalayas, the water would emerge the clear winner. Somewhere at a distance, chanting of Omkar and sounds of temple bells are touching my heart and soul. Whether the leaves have turned white because of snow fall or their color itself is white, I cannot say for sure. Some dam in the Himalayan range has cracked and submerged scores of houses. Miseries of people caught in the flood is too difficult to explain.

Water, water everywhere. In some places, it has come up to the waist level, whereas in other places it has reached the chest height. It has flooded the houses. I had heard what would happen in case of nature's fury but had not seen myself. We came here from Bombay only to save hundreds of lives. What happened that day? It was about a week or ten days since Shefali had betrayed me. Feeling bored of the hostel life. With my continuation in the hostel, her memory continued to haunt me. There was no end to my restlessness. It was at that juncture; the news of this flood came to us.

Five sisters – as the rivers were popularly called, one of them is roaring because of the flood. The water which is the backbone of people's lives has become the cause of their tears. The water from the breached dam has inundated the place submerging the houses and causing inexplicable miseries to the people. We were brought by a special plane to this place to rescue the people. Himalaya is as dangerous as its beauty. Rescue work was not as easy as we thought. If it was the river in our place, we would have jumped into the water and rescued the people. But when it comes to rivers in Himalayas, it is a different story. If we jump into the river in the biting cold, we feel our body itself may freeze. On the one side, forceful water flow. On the other, incessant rain. Many houses have already submerged in the water. How many more places are going to face the fury, cannot make out. Even amid nature's fury, the rescue operations continued. How many old lives were struggling to save themselves? How many mothers were trying to protect their children even at the cost of their lives? How many of them were mute spectators watching their children being washed away in the flood waters? Yes! Not just the human beings. Even the animals and birds were also struggling in vain. How precious is a life? I realized that day how precious it was looking at the human beings and animals screaming for help! What kind of a fool I was to have thought of sacrificing it just for the sake of love?

Anyhow, those fifteen days were literally the most significant time for all of us. The flood waters had started receding. We had shifted the rescued people to safer places. The government had arranged for their food, health, and other facilities. Our duties had also almost come to an end. The day after tomorrow, our plane was ready to leave for Bombay. Four of us came for viewing the Himalayas after taking the permission of our superior officer. I am not remembering Shefali during these moments, but of those hundreds of people who have taken shelter at the refugee camps and were trying to save their lives. I was deeply thinking of the Himalayas which has stood the test of times witnessing the lives of these people over centuries. I was living every moment admiring the Himalayas the embodiment of cleanliness, beauty, and vastness!

*****

I had returned to Bombay. The old Basya had died somewhere in the snow-covered Himalayas. What is alive now is the Basya full of new vigor, new energy, and new confidence. I was not allowing the word 'regret' to come anywhere near me as I was keeping myself fully occupied from morning to night. I have ordered my sub-conscious mind not to remind me of Shefali anytime. All that is left now is me and me alone. Sometimes, I visit the beach along with Seena. Both of us will eat whatever we get in the nearby stall, chat, and return home. The new lifestyle has enhanced my mental and physical strength, besides my enthusiasm towards the life. Four five months after returning from the Himalayas had passed just like four five minutes.

Just then the news had come as a bolt in the blue – the death of Shefali.

*****

"Hi Basya alias Basavaraj. You may change yourself to any name, I call you as Basya only. You are my life. It was like an age spending even a moment without you. I had surrendered to you the moment I saw you for the first time I say. I had become mad out of happiness when you agreed to be my friend and when you accepted my proposal. I was eagerly waiting for your training to get over so that we could start our family life. My baby which was the symbol of our love had become part of my life itself. But, when the doctor informed me of Cancer in my uterus, I lost all enthusiasm in life. On the one side, the baby had to be taken out and killed. On the other, the doctor had given me a lifespan of maximum six months. With whom shall I share my pain? In whose lap shall I rest and cry to my heart's content? I don't know. I had almost died the day the doctor took out the baby which had died in my stomach. I could not control my urge to see you once. Because of that one desire to see you, I did not commit suicide. I wanted to embrace you and kiss you the moment you reached my home. But I had decided that I should be strong. I did not want you to wash away in the flood of my love for you. How long would I survive? At the most, six months. Whereas your life is just starting. You are an idiot who does not know any tricks in life. I know how deeply you love me. I also know that you don't live even for a moment after I die. That's why I had to act like your enemy. I needed your love and certainly not you. You have shared abundant love with me which enough for my next birth also. Various tests and treatments done by the doctor was pushing me fast towards the inevitable. That chemotherapy was even more painful. Your Shefali was becoming ugly day by day due to the curse of chemotherapy. Sometimes I have screaming within myself to the throbbing pain. Did not know what to do. No amount of thanks will suffice to express my gratitude to your friend Seena who supported me in my difficult times by accompanying me from home to hospital on several occasions. I had told Seena not to tell this truth for any reason to you till my last breath. I had told him to give this letter to you after my death. So long as such friend is with you, your success is assured. Yes, I forgot to tell you. After my death you cannot waste your time in my memory. You must marry a girl and settle in life at the earliest. I will take birth as your daughter and will stay with you always. Be smiling always. Read another point carefully – I love you ten times more than Catherine's love for Jack. Love you...Basya".

- Yours Shefali.

*****

No sooner had I completed reading the letter, I lost all energies in my body and felt like collapsing. I felt disgusted about myself for having doubted and insulted Shefali. I felt ashamed of myself for failing to understand the depth of her love. My hands and legs were trembling. Without my knowledge, tears started rolling from my eyes. The letter slipped from my hands and was wet in my tears. I felt as if the earth was swallowing me, the sky was falling on me and I was getting burnt in the heat of the moment. What was the gift I gave in return to Shefali's love? She did not share her pains during her last days. She gave me happiness and suffered all the pains for herself. How much she would have felt sad over losing her baby? How many times she would have cried and how many times she would have screamed? She did not share an iota of her suffering with me. I went to Himalayas to invent myself. It was enough to look in her eyes once. I would have realized who I was. Seena, on the other hand, was looking like a giant mountain than the Himalayas. Can I value his love, patience etc.?

I feel as if I am standing atop the Himalayas. I don't have the energy to move my leg even a bit. Though I was on top of the Himalayas, my body was wet with my tears and sweat. The snow-clad Himalayas is shaking, snow is melting. Even then, I could not take a step. What kind of vastness and magnitude of that mountain? Can we survive if that mountain collapses? Though I feel like running and escaping, my hands and legs are motionless. Not able to move at all. Avalanches are becoming severe and are almost reaching my feet. That's all... The snow-covered mountain shook strongly and opened its mouth.

"With a thud, I fell down"

*****

"With a thud, I fell down"

My entire body was paining to the force of my fall. I got up and looked around. “Hey Basya! Still sleeping? Get up I say! Stupid fellow. Are you still sleeping even though the Sun has reached the mid-sky? Get up I say. Are you caught by a ghost or what? You were murmuring something like Shefali, Bombay, Military, Seena throughout the night. I don’t know what is wrong with you. Enough of dreaming, get up and clean the cow dung. Get up you lazy fellow”. Aunt’s morning chanting was heard from inside the house. I got up, washed my face in cold water and walked towards the cattle shed.

*****Shubhamastu*****

www.ingramcontent.com/pod-product-compliance
Ingram Content Group UK Ltd.
Pitfield, Milton Keynes, MK11 3LW, UK
UKHW021923190726
13853UKWH00002B/811